TAROT
ALCHEMY

TAROT
ALCHEMY

A complete analysis
of the
major arcana

KENNETH COOMBS

iUniverse, Inc.
Bloomington

TAROT ALCHEMY
A complete analysis of the major arcana

iUniverse books may be ordered through booksellers or by contacting:

iUniverse
1663 Liberty Drive
Bloomington, IN 47403
www.iuniverse.com
1-800-Authors (1-800-288-4677)

ISBN: 978-1-4697-6510-5 (sc)
ISBN: 978-1-4697-6514-3 (hc)
ISBN: 978-1-4697-6515-0 (ebk)

Library of Congress Control Number: 2012901862

Printed in the United States of America

iUniverse rev. date: 01/28/2012

CONTENTS

Introduction vii

Tarot Alchemy 1
The Four Elements.. 7
Elemental Combinations.. 10
The Seven Planets... 14
Planetary Combinations... 17
Numerology 21
The Zodiac 29
The Structure of the Tarot Deck 31
The Minor Arcana 33
The Court Cards 35
The Major Arcana... 37
Theory 51
Practice 55
Analyzing the Question 62
Methodology.. 69
Time and Timing.. 75
Some Things to Think About 78

Conclusion 83
Bibliography 201
Biography 203

INTRODUCTION

Many books have been written about the Tarot cards over the years. Most books about Tarot cards show you the image of a Tarot card and give a few sentences about what that card means or symbolizes. Some books give alternate meanings if the card is reversed. Some books give positional meanings based on where the card is located on a spread. Although it is important to know the individual meanings of the Tarot cards and their correspondences, that is not the focus of this book. Instead, I wanted to focus on the interactions of the Tarot cards with each other. This new approach of deciphering the interactions in a scientific way leads to new insights about the meanings of the Tarot cards in a reading.

There are very few books out there that discuss "blending" two different Tarot cards, which gives a richer, more specific description of events or environments in a Tarot reading. There is a synergistic effect of combining two different Tarot cards or "energies." Because I have a background in chemistry and mathematics, I have taken a scientific approach to my analysis of the Tarot cards. That is the purpose of this book. I view each of the Tarot cards as an element or molecule that reacts with another element or molecule in predictable, consistent, logical ways. By analyzing a Tarot card and breaking it down into its constituent parts and comparing it to another Tarot card, a new set of energies is described based on a logical set of rules.

I have only found a few books that discuss the topic of card combinations. These books give limited examples and do not provide a complete analysis of all possible combinations. Because there are seventy-eight Tarot cards, a complete binary analysis of the Tarot cards would consist of 3,003 combinations! This is quite a task! The Tarot cards are broken into the Major Arcana (twenty-two cards), and the Minor Arcana (fifty-six cards). It seems logical that looking at the Major Arcana first would make the most sense. This leads to 231 combinations. The Minor Arcana is further broken down into four suits corresponding to the four elements. The numbered cards represent spheres on the Tree of Life and planetary energies. In order to understand the Tarot cards, study of the Kabbalah is essential. Tarot Alchemy is a form of Kabbalah. The Minor Arcana is the result of the Alchemy of the Elements and Planets. The sixteen Court cards are part of the Minor Arcana. They represent the interactions of the four elements.

The Tarot cards represent individual energies, which can be compared to the pure elements of the period table. It is the interactions and reactions of these elements or card combinations that interest me, and these are the subject of this book. The true meaning of a reading can be determined by analyzing the components of the Tarot cards present and then applying some logical rules to determine the specific energy described. This is an accurate and precise method of analyzing the Tarot cards and answering specific questions.

My intention in writing this book was not only to make a practical reference guide but to help people learn a new methodology for understanding the language of the Tarot. This book is the result of the Tarot Alchemy I did.

The twenty-two cards of the Major Arcana represent combinations of the four elements and seven planets, and Tarot Alchemy is the process of combining the cards to reveal the message. Through the use of logic and reasonable constraints on the way questions are posed, there is no limit to the kind of information that can be obtained using Tarot cards.

Although I have used positional card spreads, such as the Tree of Life, Celtic Cross, or Pyramid, a discussion about spreads is not the focus of this book. A positional spread is more useful for general questions or no question at all. Looking at the combinations (Tarot Alchemy) of the Tarot cards in the spread can be useful and give added insight in those cases. The ability to identify patterns in the Tarot cards is an essential first step to mastering them.

Instead, this book is primarily concerned with the combinations of the Tarot cards in the Major Arcana. The Alchemy between them is important to understand. Just as in chemistry where the elements react and combine and release energy, so too the Tarot cards react with each other. Sometimes the energies of the Tarot cards cancel each other out, and their energies are unexpressed. Other times their energies and reinforced and multiplied in a synergistic way. By understanding the "thermodynamics" or energy flow in a Tarot reading, more insight can be gained in the interpretation of the message. By understanding the components present and how they interact, the answer to a specific question can be obtained through synchronicity.

An understanding of the four elements (Earth, Air, Fire, and Water) is needed in order to understand the Tarot cards and life itself. An understanding of the interactions between these four elements is also necessary! As in life, elements (like people) are combining and recombining with other elements and absorbing and releasing various energies. This is what life is all about. The shuffling of the Tarot deck is akin to the interactions of people and events. It is seemingly random and unpredictable, but as a good poker player will tell you, there are tells. By understanding the patterns in the Tarot cards, and their corresponding patterns in your life, the answers to your questions can be revealed. Once your Tarot cards are calibrated to reality, there is no limit to the insight that can be gained. I hope this book aids you on your search for truth.

TAROT ALCHEMY

So why title this book Tarot Alchemy?

Alchemy is a type of science and chemical philosophy from the Middle Ages and the renaissance that attempted to perform successful experiments of the unusual, such as trying to make gold from base metals. Alchemy is the process of taking something ordinary and turning it into something extraordinary, sometimes in a way that cannot be explained. Alchemy is a seemingly magical power or process of transmuting. It is also a form of chemistry and speculative philosophy concerned with finding an elixir of life. Alchemy is any magical power or process of transmuting a common substance, usually one of little value, into a substance of great value. Alchemy is the act of combining two seemingly unrelated things, ideas, or actions, which leads to a new third "thing" that is usually more interesting than the component parts. This is the synergistic effect.

The history of the Tarot cards is well documented. I suggest you read many books about the Tarot cards as it will help you build up an image of what the energy represents in the real world. Because the individual Tarot cards represent distinct energies or energy combinations, the process of combining two Tarot cards and analyzing the result is called Tarot Alchemy.

Just as matter and the elements of the periodic table follow the laws of chemistry, the Tarot cards follow the laws of spiritual chemistry. Because the Tarot represents different combinations of planetary and elemental forces, it is possible to determine the meaning of card interactions in addition to individual card meanings.

Life is the result of the Alchemy of spirit and matter. The Tarot cards are the language of that interaction. When the four elements are balanced manifestation is possible. When the seven planets are balanced spirit is created. The Tarot is a reflection of life.

Tarot Alchemy, when understood, can be applied to the "real world" as well.

Growing up, I always had an interest in computers. I also liked Tarot cards. It wasn't until I combined these two different attributes of my character that my Tarot website (sunmoontarot.com) was created. By combining two seemingly different areas of my life, a new third energy was created. This led to my becoming a professional Tarot card reader serving clients all over the world. Tarot cards are not as useful without people! It takes people to create the Tarot cards, shuffle them, consult them and analyze them. Just as in life. Tarot Alchemy led to the creation of this book!

The principles of Tarot Alchemy can be applied to any Tarot spread. Tarot cards should be read in pairs to understand the type of energy defined as well as the speed, the intensity, and the direction of the energy flow. The understanding of how to answer a question posed by a client is essential. The ability to determine timing is essential to have when interpreting a Tarot reading, as many questions that clients ask are concerned as to when an event might take place or when they should take action for success. Tarot Alchemy can reveal the methods to determine times in a very precise, accurate way. The use of Tarot Alchemy in a Tarot reading and in life can help you be a better interpreter of truth.

By keeping records of Tarot readings and real world outcomes, the Tarot deck can be calibrated to reality. When something unusual happens, I like to try and determine which planets, elements and numerology might describe that situation and from that determine which Tarot cards or Tarot card combinations might describe that situation accurately. For example what if I saw a very angry pregnant woman driving a car recklessly? The Tarot card combination that might describe this would be The Tower, The Empress and The Chariot.

The Empress is the pregnant woman, the Tower can be her anger and the Chariot points to the car she is driving. By thinking in this way, it is easier to decipher a Tarot reading. It is sometimes useful to work backwards when analyzing a Tarot card spread and calibrate their meanings to reality. Describe a situation in terms of planets and elements and determine which Tarot cards would point to that situation.

When two molecules react, they either release or absorb energy. The same is true with the Tarot cards. When two Tarot cards are combined, they either release or absorb energy. This leads to an active or passive nature. This adds information about the flow of energy in a Tarot spread. Some Tarot combinations are positive (constructive) and others negative (destructive). Recognizing the details of these interactions is the goal of Tarot Alchemy as this leads to detail in a Tarot spread. The information gained through Tarot Alchemy should be useful in any type of Tarot reading or spread.

The cards drawn are the elements, and the interactions and combinations of these cards reveal the details and answer the question. This is Tarot Alchemy, combining two different energies to create a new third energy.

Tarot Alchemy gives you the ability to read your environment and deduce what it means. Understanding the colors and shapes and sizes of objects around you, can give you a clue as to what will happen. Perception is the intersection of thought and time.

What if you are watching TV and you see a picture of a Corvette. Well, your friend Steve has a Corvette. All of a sudden, the phone rings, and it is Steve on the other end! Well, did the TV cause Steve to call? Did the TV change your thoughts? Did you cause the Corvette to appear on the TV? Did you cause Steve to call you by thinking about him? Did Steve cause all of this to happen prior to his call? Was Steve affected by the TV?

All of these questions may seem unrelated, but in reality, they are connected! All of these interactions are valid. Time is the intersection point between events. This is connected to the laws of causality and synchronicity.

Consider the following example of Tarot Alchemy and hidden connections between Tarot cards. The Hierophant (5) plus The Tower (16). The Hierophant is Venus, but shows numerology linked to Mars. The Tower is Mars, but shows numerology linked to Venus. Because of this, these two particular Tarot cards would strengthen each other in a Tarot reading. The study of these 'hidden' connections gives rise to detail in a Tarot reading linked to reality. The ability to see specifics is possible using the principles of Tarot Alchemy.

So you see, even a Tarot card that represents Mars expresses Venus, and the Tarot card that is Venus expresses Mars. Sometimes the opposite potential energy of a Tarot card is expressed in itself. Knowledge of numerology, kabbalah and astrology is useful when studying the interactions of the Tarot cards with each other.

What about the Empress card? The Empress is ruled by planet Venus, but it may not be apparent at first that there is a linkage to planet Saturn. The Empress card is number three and three = Saturn. Without understanding numerology, this hidden connection might have been missed. Since The Empress card is connected to Saturn, it is strengthened by any other Saturn card that should appear next to it. For example, the World Card, The Devil and The Star card all point to Saturn. When they show up combined with the Empress, the connection is stronger. It is like comparing different kinds of molecular bonds in molecules. Some bonds are strong and some are weak. Some molecules repel each other. So too do the Tarot cards.

Relative proportions of elements and planets in a Tarot spread should be analyzed. I have attempted a scientific explanation of the results in my analysis of the card combinations. I believe that a logical scientific analysis is necessary to avoid subjectivity in a tarot reading. All of the twenty-two Tarot cards in the Major Arcana are linked to one another in many different ways. They can be connected by elements. For example, the Hermit and the Devil both share the Earth element. Cards may also be linked by planet. For example, the Empress and Justice cards both share the planet Venus. They may also be linked through numerology. The Tower and the Chariot are linked by the number seven, and in numerology, seven equals sixteen, which points to the Tower. There can also be other connections. For example, the Chariot card is number Seven, and the number seven represents Venus, so this could be linked to the Justice card, which is ruled by Venus. So you see there are hidden connections between Tarot cards in the Major Arcana that must be understood. If two cards share an attribute, it generally means that it is a favorable or strong pairing. This is important to consider when analyzing a Tarot spread.

In order to understand connections between Tarot cards, it is important to be familiar with the overall structure of the Tarot deck. This will enable you to spot patterns in the cards with more ease. The seventy-eight cards in the Tarot deck give rise to millions of combinations that reflect reality. By using the laws of Tarot Alchemy the message can be systematically revealed.

The structure of the Tarot deck is based on the principles of the four elements, seven planets and twelve signs of the Zodiac (which is merely combinations of planet and element). These forces combine and recombine with each other to create the complete Tarot deck. Knowledge of the four elements and seven planets is essential to understand the message contained in the cards. There are many books on these topics so seek out as much knowledge on these topics as you can. I have included a basic description of these forces here.

THE FOUR ELEMENTS

Why four elements? The periodic table of the elements contains 117 elements.

The traditional four elements are Earth, Air, Fire and Water. Of course, the 117 elements all fall into one of these groups. The four elements represent the states of matter, solid, liquid and gas, with heat being necessary to transform one to the other.

The four elements correspond to the four bases of DNA essential for life. The four elements represent the four seasons. Much has been written about the four elements and it is essential to understand the basics of what each of the four represent and how to recognize their patterns in everyday life.

Air represents thought. Water is the emotions. Fire is the behaviors. Earth represents matter and physical objects. It is the manifestation process from idea, through motivation and behavior to final result. It is the act of magic. When the four elements are balanced, life is the result. Our bodies represent the union of the four elements. Our dependence on oxygen (Air), Water, Heat, and food all demonstrate this spiritual principle

The ability to identify what element a Tarot card represents is essential. In the Minor Arcana, it is easy to know what element a Tarot card references. That is the four suits: Wands (Fire), Cups (Water), Swords (Air), and Pentacles (Earth). There are no suits in the Major Arcana, so knowledge of the Zodiac is needed to determine what element a Tarot card represents.

Some Tarot cards strengthen or weaken each other. Their energy is expressed in the form of waves that either cancel each other out or reinforce one another. The duality (a result of balance and karma) is the reason that the four elements (Tetragrammaton, the four letter name of God YHVH) balance each other. When the four elements are balanced, usually through the rotation of the Wheel of Fortune, spiritual energy is created and manifestation is possible. Karma is the result of the spinning of the Wheel of Fortune. There are different kinds of karma as well. Intellectual, emotional, behavioral and material karma all correspond to the four elements.

Here are some basic meanings of the four elements:

Earth: Matter. Practicality, stability, materialism, money and realism. Earth is nature and long-lasting structures. Capricorn, Taurus, and Virgo (the Devil, the Hierophant, and the Hermit). Physical objects, careers, finances, the physical body. Earth equals matter, the physical elements, and the rules of nature. Earth represents gravity and the physical objects. Pentacles. The Page of Pentacles and Ace of Pentacles represent the pure Earth element.

Air: Thought. Mental processes, language, intellect, reason, communication, ideas, mathematics, Gemini, Libra, and Aquarius (the Lovers, Justice, and the Star). The breath of life. Sharing our thoughts with others. The transfer of ideas through communication. Air equals thoughts and ideas. Air represents the higher consciousness and the potential self. Swords. The Knight of Swords and Ace of Swords represent the pure Air element.

Fire: Behavior. Passion, energy, impulse, inspiration, faith, creative energy. Heat and light. The energy behind a good relationship. Fire represents impulsive behavior. Or a time of passion. Aries, Leo, and Sagittarius (the Emperor, Strength, and Temperance). Fire equals behaviors and things that change or evolve. Wands. The King of Wands and Ace of Wands represent the pure Fire element.

Water: Emotion. Nurturing, intuition, dreams, psychic energy. Pisces, Cancer and Scorpio (the Moon, the Chariot, and Death) are connected to the element of Water. A natural connection to deeper truths. Natural rhythms. Our connection to the greater universe. Instincts and intuitions. The ability to understand the symbols of synchronicity. Water equals motions and love relationships. Cups. The Queen of Cups and Ace of Cups represent the pure Water element.

The following table shows the connection between element and the signs of the Zodiac.

Earth	Dry	Cold	Passive	Pages	Objects	Pentacles	Capricorn, Taurus, Virgo
Air	Wet	Hot	Active	Knights	Thoughts	Swords	Aquarius, Gemini, Libra
Fire	Dry	Hot	Active	Kings	Actions	Wands	Aries, Leo, Sagittarius
Water	Wet	Cold	Passive	Queens	Emotions	Cups	Pisces, Cancer, Scorpio

In addition to understanding the four elements, it is also important to understand their interactions with each other. Tarot Alchemy on the four elements leads to six combinations.

ELEMENTAL COMBINATIONS

It is important to understand the combinations of the four elements in a Tarot reading. For example, the presence of a Water card and a Fire card in close proximity in a Tarot spread would tend to cancel each other out, and their energies will be unexpressed. In a reading with lots of Fire and Air, there would be a bright, hot flame. An analysis of the four elements and their interactions with each other is needed in a Tarot reading.

For example, Air strengthens Fire, and Air can be heated by Fire. Fire destroys Earth but can be suffocated by Earth as well. Water can be heated by fire and turned to steam, or water can put out the flames.

When Ice is heated, it becomes liquid. When the liquid is heated, it becomes steam. Ice equals Earth, which equals the Pentacles. Liquid equals Water, which equals the Cups. Steam equals Air, which equals the Swords. The Fire element (Wands) is the heat that transmutes one to the other. Earth changes to Water and then changes to Air as it is heated by Fire. All of these elemental changes take place in the realm of the vacuum, ether, or spiritual world. When the four elements are balanced, spirit, light, and life are created and manifestation is possible.

Some elements like Fire and Air benefit each other. Water and Earth are compatible but a bit passive at times. Once the water falls down the waterfall, new energy is needed to keep the motion. Earth and Air create dust.

In the Tarot deck, The Kings are Fire, the Queens are Water, the Knights are Air, and the Pages are Earth. The Wands are Fire, the Cups are Water, The Swords are Air and the Pentacles are Earth. There are four elements, so there are sixteen ways to combine them. These sixteen combinations correspond to the Court cards in the Minor Arcana.

The connection between the Court cards and the elemental combinations is discussed in the Court Cards section of this book. The main point is that the court cards are the binary combinations of the four elements. By looking at the suit and the rank of the card, it is possible to define two elements. For example the Page of Swords is Air + Earth. The Queen of Cups is Water + Water. By looking at the combination of elements inherent in the card, it is possible to decipher its true meaning.

Here is my brief analysis of the combination of elemental forces:

Earth + Air = Dust and smoke. Caves or gases trapped in solids. Porous stones. Airplanes. It is the connection between thought and matter. It can be the manifestation of thought. New ideas that spring from things you see or touch. It can also be the environment around you that is changing your thoughts. Page of Swords and Knight of Pentacles.

Earth + Fire = Lava. Molten metals. Solids that are melted or burned by Fire. Earth can smother a Fire. The fuel (carbon) needed by fire. It is the connection between matter and motion. It is behaviors connected to manifestation. It is the motion of the physical body. Walking or running. Matter or situations that alter behavior. Page of Wands and King of Pentacles.

Earth + Water = A lake, river, or island. Water can be contained by Earth. Water can dissolver Earth. Earth can absorb water. Erosion. The water that created the Grand Canyon. The connection between emotions and matter. An object that elicits an emotional response. Manifestations that are the result of purely emotional energies. An intense emotional response to an object. Page of Cups and Queen of Pentacles.

Air + Fire = A strong combination. It is the Air needed by Fire. Fire is the result of combing Air and Earth. This reaction actually shows that Fire creates Water! Methane and oxygen yield carbon dioxide and water. The connection between thought and behavior. Taking action on your thoughts. The use of logic and knowledge. Intentional activity. Behavior that affects thought. Thought that affects behavior. Knight of Wands and King of Swords.

Air + Water = Clouds or bubbles or gases dissolved in liquids. Carbonated beverages. These elements like to stay apart or away from each other. Clouds become rain or even snow. Gases bubble out of liquids. The connection between thought and emotion. When you are in a highly emotional state, it is difficult to think clearly. Sometimes when one is too logical, it is hard to be compassionate. Logic applied with intuition. Knight of Cups and Queen of Swords.

Fire + Water = It may be counterintuitive, but Fire actually creates Water. Water creates life. Therefore, Fire creates life. If Earth and Air create Fire and therefore life, then Air (thought) and Earth (result of thought) is the intention of life. So perhaps if I want to manifest a thought, this combination is the fuel. I need the heat and light (Fire to create the Water). Fire is the process of manifestation. The connection between behavior and emotion. Emotional motivations. Emotions that cause behavioral change. Fight or flight. King of Cups and Queen of Wands.

These combinations of the four elements are connected to the I Ching, also called Book of Changes. The I Ching is a Chinese book of ancient origin consisting of sixty-four interrelated hexagrams along with commentaries attributed to Confucius. The hexagrams, originally used for divination, embody Taoist philosophy by describing all nature and human endeavor in terms of the interaction of yin and yang. It is a binary system of divination in which trigrams give rise to hexagrams. There are sixty-four hexagrams in the I Ching system. The various combinations of the four elements lead to the trigrams and hexagrams of the I Ching. It is a binary system of divination. Computers are binary. Perhaps the I Ching was an ancient computer.

Understanding the natural flow of energy from one element to the other is essential when analyzing a Tarot reading or life itself. Most people think that Fire and Water are enemies, but one unusual fact that people may not realize is that Fire actually *creates* Water. This may be unexpected, but the laws of chemistry demonstrate this truth. Fire is nothing more than an oxidation reaction. This is a very common type of reaction in chemistry. $CH_4 + 2(O_2) = CO_2 + 2(H_2O)$

The CH_4 is the Earth element, the fuel. The O_2 is the Air element. The CO_2 represents the Fire element, and Water is the result. Light and heat are also given off. When the four elements are combined, the light (spirit) is the result.

Understanding the interplay and hidden connections between the four elements leads to great detail in deciphering a Tarot card spread.

In addition to understanding the four elements and the subtleties of their interactions, the seven planets must also be studied.

THE SEVEN PLANETS

Because the twenty-two cards of the Major Arcana are merely the combinations of the four elements and seven planets, an understanding of these eleven forces is necessary to understand the interactions of the cards.

Why seven planets? I thought there were nine planets? Wait a minute; the moon is not a planet. The sun is not a planet. This doesn't make sense!

Well, in the language of Tarot, the sun and moon are considered planetary forces. The seven traditional planetary forces are Saturn, Jupiter, Mars, Sun, Venus, Mercury, and Moon. These correspond to the seven days of the week. Obviously Earth is a planet, but it is not included in the seven. What about Neptune, Pluto and Uranus? Well, there is some debate as to whether these are planets at all. Because they are so far out in the solar system, their effect on humans is diminished. These seven planetary forces are expressed and interact on Earth by humans. Life is necessary to experience the interactions of the seven planets. Perception is necessary for reality and manifestation.

It is important to understand the seven classic planetary forces and their interactions with each other to understand the message in a Tarot spread. Again, the individual planetary meanings are important, but the interactions of the forces give detail and insight in a Tarot reading.

Planet	Keywords	Day of the Week	Color	Metals
Saturn	Time	Saturday	Black	Lead
Jupiter	Construction	Thursday	Blue	Tin
Mars	Destruction	Tuesday	Red	Iron
Sun	Growth / Energy	Sunday	Yellow	Gold
Venus	Love / Art / Nature	Friday	Green	Copper
Mercury	Science / Communication	Wednesday	Orange	Mercury
Moon	Spiritual Awareness	Monday	Purple	Silver

Here are some terms that may help you understand the nature of a particular planetary energy:

Saturn: Time, old things, slow-moving things, obstacles, cemeteries, the densest form of matter. Gravity, contempt, decay, the elderly, frustrations, gloom, hibernation, humility, ice, isolation, jails, mining, mountains, privacy, regression, regularity, rejection, remorse, selfishness, shadows, silence, statues, old trees, unhappy, unlucky, watches, weights of measure, wells, winter. The Devil, The Star, The World.

Jupiter: Abundance, accumulation, achievement, awards, benefactors, blessings, castles, civilization, clothing, coats, ethics, wheat fields, good fortune, friendship, financial gain, gluttony, mercy, politeness, profit, reason, respect, riches, scriptures, self-esteem, stores, taxation, temples, wealth, wisdom. The Moon, Temperance, Wheel of Fortune.

Mars: Destruction, male, accidents, alcohol, ambition, arguments, military, arrows, assault, blacksmiths, boxing, burns, crime, danger, energy, fire, iron, knives, murder, noise, guns, poisons, red, cuts, savages, scorpions, tobacco, weapons. Death, The Emperor, The Tower.

Sun: Growth, energy, life, achievement, prosperity, abundance, light, ego, gold, honor, individuality, leaders, noon, popularity, pride, royalty, wisdom. Yellow, vitality, publicity, importance, power, lions, lemons, horse, daytime and confidence. Strength, The Sun.

Venus: Love, art, music, beauty, ballet, brides, cats, clothing, companions, copper, courtships, desire, doves, elegance, emeralds, equality, fashion, females, flattery, flowers, fragrance, friendship, gardens, grapes, marriage, mother, perfume, plants, polite, roses, society, songs. The Empress, The Hierophant, Justice.

Mercury: Accountants, written agreements, numbers, communication, logic, mathematics, science, chemistry, authors, bisexual, brain, computers, telephones, travel, diaries, dictionaries, doctors, education, grammar, interviews, logic, memory, pencils, quizzes, reading, research, science, teachers, transportation, vision, voice. The Hermit, The Lovers, The Magician.

Moon: Intuition, psychic or spiritual energy, visions, mirrors, cycles, baptism, bathing, swimming, boats, childbirth, crabs, dew, dogs and wolves, emotions, fish, fluids, fungus, glass, insomnia, lakes, water lilies, milk, night, oysters, pearls, rain, reproduction, romance, rivers, sea, silver, tides, water, womb. The High Priestess, The Chariot.

Or course the individual planetary meanings are necessary, but the combinations of the planetary forces give added insight and detail in a Tarot reading.

PLANETARY COMBINATIONS

Here are all of the binary combinations of the seven planets. There are twenty-one different combinations that should be examined.

Saturn and Jupiter: Time and construction. Buildings and other establishments that stand the test of time. The role of time in the creative process. Stable, long-term success. Creativity and achievement. Realizing a goal and overcoming challenges.

Saturn and Mars: Time and destruction. Erosion. Death comes to all in time. Long periods of destruction. Aggression and aggressive behaviors. Negative patterns of behavior. Addictions and self-destructive behavior. All great empires will fall. Time conquers all.

Saturn and Sun: Time and growth; energy and longevity. A long cycle of abundance. Gaining knowledge and wisdom through experience. The ability to predict the future and understand the truth of the past. The mind always has the ability to time travel. Only perceived light is visible.

Saturn and Venus: Time and love. A love that stands the test of time. A long-lasting, loving relationship. Can be a long-distance relationship of love. Old artwork and the beauty of old objects and statues. Can be obstacles that a love relationship must overcome.

Saturn and Mercury: Time and communication. The use of logic to analyze the behavior of others. Communication with someone who is far away. Thought can travel through time. Send yourself a message to the future. It takes time for a thought to materialize. If you understand the factors that control that time lag, then manifestations can be done more efficiently.

Saturn and Moon: Time and intuition and emotions. Seeing visions of the future. The spirit can travel through time. The intuition can sense the future before it happens. Activity at night is indicated. Traditions and culture.

Jupiter and Mars: Construction and destruction. A stalemate. A strong defender battling a strong opponent. Their energies are equal, so no progress is made. This is the conflict that keeps the balance. It is the Democrats fighting the Republicans.

Jupiter and Sun: Construction and growth and energy. Good ideas and plans that will be carried out. A designer or architect. A positive, creative person. Success and prosperity due to quality work. Wealth and gold.

Jupiter and Venus: Construction and love. Working on a marriage. Building a strong foundation for a relationship. A positive, stable relationship of love. A defender of love and romance.

Jupiter and Mercury: Construction and communication. A creative and intellectual accomplishment. Writing a book or solving a problem. Using mathematics to create. The use of knowledge to help others. An architect.

Jupiter and Moon: Construction and intuition and emotions. Having a dream. Motivation for change. An emotional response to an accomplishment. Giving and receiving praise. Emotional connections to accomplishments.

Mars and Sun: Destruction and growth and energy. The temple must be destroyed before it can be rebuilt. Bad habits and aggression can be healed. Good triumphs over evil. A vital, aggressive energy. Strong and conquering.

Mars and Venus: Destruction and love. The classic male-female, love-hate battle of the sexes. It is the union of opposites. The union of the male and female energy necessary for the conception of a person or idea.

Mars and Mercury: Destruction and communication; confusion and cognitive distortions. Logic blinded by rage. Impulsive behaviors based on miscommunication. The use of logic and science in a competitive way. Military science.

Mars and Moon: Destruction and intuition and emotions. Irrational and aggressive emotions. Bad dreams and self-destructive, obsessive-compulsive behaviors. A disconnect between behavior and motivation. Confusion and the unconscious mind or passive-aggressive behavior.

Sun and Venus: Growth and energy and love. Good health, life, birth, and vitality. Gold and success. Art, beauty, and strength. Love and abundance. Blessings of all kinds. A very fortunate combination.

Sun and Mercury: Growth and energy and communication. Success of mind. The ability to achieve your desires. Accomplishment and recognition. Skill and ability. Fame and wisdom.

Sun and Moon: Growth and energy and intuition and emotion. Spiritual revelation. Knowledge of God and your spiritual gifts. Understanding the messages of the mind. The union of the left and right sides of the brain. The eclipse. A very powerful, mysterious energy.

Venus and Mercury: Love and communication. Understanding beauty and art. Analysis of art and nature. The mathematical or practical side of beauty or art. The union of art and science. The beauty of numbers and geometric forms. The logical aspect of a love relationship.

Venus and Moon: Love and intuition and emotions. A very romantic combination that leads to pregnancy. The emotional fulfillment of a love relationship. Intimacy in the love relationship.

Mercury and Moon: Communication and intuition and emotions. The analysis of symbols and understanding foreign languages. The ability to use intuition with wisdom and logical constructs. Making sense of spiritual energy. Communication with the spirit world. A spiritual medium.

In addition to understanding the four elements, the seven planets and all of their combinations, it is essential to understand the role of numbers and numerology in the interpretations of messages from the Tarot cards.

NUMEROLOGY

Add, subtract, multiply, divide, behold! The language of Tarot cards is mathematics and numbers. Numerology is the study of numbers, namely the meanings of the numbers zero through nine. The sequence of the letters in the North American alphabet is the key to understanding their meaning. It is not by accident that A = 1, B = 2, C = 3. The Major Arcana of the Tarot cards all have numbers on them. The numbers also correspond to planets and letters of the alphabet. Every number is a name, and every name is a number. Because numbers never lie, an objective and precise answer can be given to a question. Numbers are everywhere in life, so understanding the meaning of numbers can help in all areas of your life.

In order to analyze a Tarot reading properly, knowledge of numerology is important. Knowledge of numerology can help you in many areas of your life, not just Tarot readings. Understanding patterns in the Tarot cards can help you see patterns in the corresponding 'real world'. Knowing what messages the numbers around you may be sending can give clues as to how to take action for a successful result. By using the laws of mathematics, new insights can be determined objectively in a Tarot reading. There is no guesswork involved, and questions can be answered quickly and effectively. In general even numbers are passive (female) and odd numbers are active (male).

I have included some basic information about numerology here. Again, I suggest you do your own research on this topic to strengthen your interpretation skills.

1	2	3	4	5	6	7	8	9
A	B	C	D	E	F	G	H	I
J	K	L	M	N	O	P	Q	R
S	T	U	V	W	X	Y	Z	
Male	Female	Saturn	Jupiter	Mars	Sun	Venus	Mercury	Moon

Numbers correspond to the Planetary forces. By understanding which numbers correspond to which planetary force, new information can be revealed and insight gained. So how does numerology work? The basic idea is that any number can be reduced down to one digit by adding the digits together. For example, $14 = 1 + 4 = 5$. Or $2381 = 2 + 3 + 8 + 1 = 14 = 1 + 4 = 5$. So if you are given a number, of course the individual digits will tell a story, the Alchemy between them also tells a story, but the final one digit that is obtained determines what energy rules them all. So, if I have the number 135 which adds to 9, then the number 9 (Moon) is the ruler of this number.

Knowing which energies are associated with each number enables you to decipher the message behind it. If a person wanted to buy a house and had two houses in mind, numerology can be used to reveal which house is the better choice. For example if the house numbers of the two choices were 535 and 460, what could this reveal about which one would be a better choice?

First examine the individual meanings of the numbers involved. In house number 535, the 5 and 3 show up and point to Mars and Saturn. This can point to a house in danger of burning! It is a dark place and cold. If you add up the numbers 535 this adds to 13. This number points to the Death card in the Tarot! House number 460 = points to Jupiter and Sun. These are both fortunate planets. The $4 + 6 = 10$ and points to the Wheel of Fortune. Also, zeros are good to have in a number because it points to the influence of spirit. Clearly the best choice of houses would be house number 460.

Words can be analyzed in a similar way by converting the letters into numbers. In my experience over the years, I have found that the strongest influence is actually the first letter of the word or name. This is the first sound the brain hears when it is associated with an object. This usually reveals the outward nature of the energy. For example the word Karma = k = 11 = Justice = equality. The "equals sign" is an 11 turned on its side. Karma = balance and true justice.

There is a difference between vowels and consonants too. Normally, vowels represent your inner nature, while the consonants represent your outer self and persona. There are many good books about numerology out there, so I suggest a firm knowledge of numerology if you want to sharpen your skills in a Tarot card analysis.

Every name is a number and every number is a name. Numerology can be used to analyze names also. For example, my name is Kenneth. When you substitute the numbers in for the letters, you will get the following sequence: 2 5 5 5 5 2 8. Add them up and the total is 32. For the word "chemist", the sequence is: 3 8 5 4 9 1 2. This total is also 32. Maybe it is not by accident that I am a chemist!

Numerology is the language of the Tarot. There are seventy-eight Tarot cards. Seventy-eight is an interesting number because it is the addition of the numbers one through twelve. This represents the twelve signs of the Zodiac. Therefore, the entire deck of Tarot cards can be laid out in a perfect pyramid. I have a developed a Tarot spread based on this information. You can read more about that on my website: www.sunmoontarot.com/pyramid.html.

In order to understand Tarot cards, knowledge of numerology is important. Each Tarot card of the Major Arcana is assigned a number from zero to twenty-one for a total of twenty-two cards. Remember that in numerology, a two-digit number is added together until there is only one digit left. This defines the true nature of the energy.

Numbers describe different types of energy. Light is broken down into wavelengths and frequency. This is proportional to energy. Different colors have different wavelengths and frequencies and therefore have different energies. Short wavelengths have high energy. I will give some basic information in the following table.

#	Planet	Keywords	Colors	Letters	Months	Years
1	Male	Active, conscious, new, independent, creative	White	A J S	January, October	2008
2	Female	Passive, unconscious, intuitive, innocent	Grey	B K T	February, November	2009
3	Saturn	Time, obstacles, delays, stability matter	Black	C L U	March, December	2010
4	Jupiter	Creative, constructive, protective, beneficial	Blue	D M V	April	2011
5	Mars	Angry, destructive, impulsive, authority	Red	E N W	May	2012
6	Sun	Positive energy, growth, healing, optimism	Yellow	F O X	June	2013
7	Venus	Love, music, beauty, art, nature, relationships	Green	G P Y	July	2014
8	Mercury	Science, logic, healing, communication	Orange	H Q Z	August	2015
9	Moon	Psychic energy, ghosts and spirits, unseen energy	Purple	I R	September	2016

By applying the laws of numerology, letters can be determined using the Major Arcana, and words and names can even be spelled. For example, if a client asks, "What will be the first name of my next husband?" Three Major Arcana are drawn, and the cards drawn include The Emperor (4), The Magician (1), and Temperance (14).

Notice that the numbers associated with these cards are four, one, and fourteen respectively. Since 4 = D, 1 = A, and 14 = N, this spells out the word "Dan!" This is an extreme example, and usually, it is difficult to form a name out of three Tarot cards; however, the first letter of the first name or initials can be revealed easily.

Another example of the use of numerology in a Tarot reading is as follows: If a woman asks how many children she will give birth to in her life and the three Tarot cards are The Empress (3), The High Priestess (2), and The Star (17).

The numbers present are three, two, and seventeen respectively. Although there is a chance that seventeen children are possible, the likely answer is either two or three. A bit of common sense is sometimes needed when one is analyzing Tarot cards. These numbers (and corresponding letters) all have their own unique energy. By understanding that energy, it can be controlled, directed, and combined with other energies to manifest your future in the ways you see fit. This is the true meaning of the Magician in the Tarot deck. The Magician has the ability to turn thought into reality, specifically the ability to assemble the four elements, balance them, and call upon the spiritual energy to manifest his thought into physical form. The result of this magic (manifestation process) is fire, which creates light and water. Water then creates life. By understanding what energies you have at your disposal (and when to use them), manifestation will happen more efficiently and lead you to peace of mind. Using the power of numbers can reveal specifics and levels of understanding that may be unexpected. Give the breath of life to your ideas, and they will come to pass. If you know how to analyze the elements, planets, and numerology present in a Tarot reading, a more precise picture of the results will be revealed. The principles of Tarot Alchemy can help you interpret different aspects of your life and aid in the decision making process. The goal of a Tarot reading is to reveal truth, after all, so understanding all of the components and how they interrelate is essential to understanding the complete message from the Tarot cards. Knowledge of the four elements, the seven planets, and numerology is essential.

Consider the following example: What if I asked the Tarot cards, "What will the winning Powerball numbers be on such and such a date?" The three Major Arcana are Strength (8), the Sun (19), and the Devil (15).

The corresponding numbers are 8, 19, and 15. Perhaps other combinations of these numbers are needed. For example: 8 + 19 = 27. 8 + 15 = 23. 19 + 15 = 34. If you add up all three corresponding numbers, you get 42. Perhaps 8, 15, 19, 23, 27, 34, and 42 would all be good numbers to play!

Consider another example: What if a client asked the question, "Which man should I marry, Steven or William?" If the three Tarot cards chosen were the Wheel of Fortune (10), the Sun (19), and the Star (17), we get the numbers 10, 19, and 17.

The letters are J, S, and Q. Because the letter S = Steven, then Steven is the clear objective answer. Simple! If a woman asked, "What will be the name of my next husband?" and the three Tarot cards were the Emperor (4), the Moon (18), and the High Priestess (2), the following letters would be indicated: D, M, V, I, R, B, K, and T. His first name will start with one of those letters. David, Michael, Vincent, Isaac, Richard, Brian, Kenneth, Tyler all are possible! Perhaps all the letters are needed. What about Tim, Dirk, Dmitri or Kirk?

THE ZODIAC

The twelve signs of the Zodiac are the result of combining Planets and Elements. It is the Alchemy of the Planets and Elements. If there are four elements and seven planets, there are 28 different combinations possible. Why are there only 12 Zodiac signs? Where are the other 16 Interactions? Well, they are expressed in the Minor Arcana. For Example, the Sun + Earth is not expressed in the Zodiac, but is expressed in the Minor Arcana as the 6 of Pentacles. The study of Astrology can give insight in the analysis of a Tarot reading. Astrology is the study of planetary Alchemy.

Zodiac	Planet	Element	Tarot Trump
Aries	Mars	Fire	The Emperor (4)
Taurus	Venus	Earth	The Hierophant (5)
Gemini	Mercury	Air	The Lovers (6)
Cancer	Moon	Water	The Chariot (7)
Leo	Sun	Fire	Strength (8)
Virgo	Mercury	Earth	The Hermit (9)
Libra	Venus	Air	Justice (11)
Scorpio	Mars	Water	Death (13)
Sagittarius	Jupiter	Fire	Temperance (14)
Capricorn	Saturn	Earth	The Devil (15)
Aquarius	Saturn	Air	The Star (17)
Pisces	Jupiter	Water	The Moon (18)

If you add up the numbers from 1 to 12, the result is 78, the number of the Tarot cards. This is a powerful number that leads to a perfect pyramid arrangement of the entire Tarot deck. Read about the Pyramid Tarot reading here:

http://www.SunMoonTarot.com/pyramid.html

In a Tarot reading it is important to know some basic information about the people involved in the questions. For example it is good to know the Zodiac sign of the client. Once a Zodiac sign is known, a Tarot card from the Court cards can be assigned to that person. For example, if someone where a Libra male, then the Tarot card would be King or Knight of Swords. Or if they are a female Cancer, then they would be the Queen or Page of cups. When the Court cards show up in a Tarot reading, it is easy to know who is who if the Zodiac signs are known.

THE STRUCTURE OF THE TAROT DECK

It is important to understand the structure of the Tarot deck in order to analyze a reading properly. Knowing that the four suits in the Minor Arcana represent the four elements and their numbered values represent the spheres on the Tree of Life and the planetary forces is very important in understanding the Tarot. By knowing which planets and elements are connected to each Tarot card, the reading will give insight into the message given by the Tarot cards.

The structure of the Tarot cards, just like the universe is fractal. There are a total of seventy-eight Tarot cards. There are twenty-two Major Arcana cards corresponding to the twenty-two letters of the Hebrew alphabet. Furthermore, the Major Arcana is broken down into seven Planetary cards, twelve Zodiac cards, and three Elemental cards. There are fifty-six Minor Arcana cards further divided into the forty numbered cards and the sixteen Court cards (Kings, Queens, Knights and Pages). The sixteen court cards represent the interactions of the four elements with each other. The Minor Arcana consists of four suits of fourteen cards. Modern day playing cards are derived from Tarot cards. There are no Major Arcana cards in the modern playing card deck. There are also no Pages. Diamonds = Pentacles, Hearts = Cups, Spades = Swords and Clubs = Wands. So remember, the next time you are playing poker or blackjack in a casino, you are really playing with the Tarot cards!

In order to analyze a Tarot card interaction properly, some basic information about the structure of the Tarot deck must be known. Most students of Tarot know the basics. For example, these individuals will know that Wands equal Fire, Cups equal Water, Swords equal Air, and

Pentacles equal Earth. This book is written for the advanced student of Tarot, the one who is ready to go to the next level in Tarot analysis. I will briefly describe the general structure of the entire Tarot deck, but my focus here is on the Major Arcana, a special group of twenty-two Tarot cards that represent the twenty-two letters of the Hebrew alphabet. It is important to study kabbalah to understand the structure of the Tarot deck. The ten numbered cards represent the ten spheres on the Tree of Life, while the cards of the Major Arcana represent the twenty-two pathways between them all. I recommend a book called The Qabalistic Tarot by Robert Wang. It describes the structure of the Tarot in elemental and planetary terms and gives a lot of useful information.

The Structure of the Tarot is fractal, just as an atom can be decomposed into smaller and smaller particles, the Tarot deck is broken down into smaller and smaller subsets that finally result in a pure energy. The act of deconstructing the composition of two different Tarot cards and reconstructing them with the new combination of energies gives rise to a new 'molecule', with a discreet specific energy that is different than the two cards alone. This is the process of Tarot Alchemy and leads to insight. Energy is either absorbed or emitted during this process. Some sets of Tarot cards are bonded to each other strongly, for example two earth sign cards like Hierophant and Hermit, and other card combinations repel each other like The Moon (Water) and Strength (Fire).

Understanding the structure of the Tarot deck can lead to insights about the structure of your life. The two main groups of cards in the Tarot deck are the Minor and Major Arcana. The Minor Arcana represents the external, material world. The Major Arcana represents forms of spiritual energy and the internal world. Understanding the flow of energy between these two worlds can aid you in your decision making process.

THE MINOR ARCANA

I am not going to spend a lot of time on the Minor Arcana in this book. There are many books that can give you the individual card meanings of these fifty-six cards. A card from the Minor Arcana is a combination of Element and Planet. The Court cards are Element-Element interactions. The numbered cards correspond to spheres on the Tree of Life and are connected to numerology, alphabets, mathematics and language. The fifty-six cards of the Minor Arcana represent the four elements. It is essential to understand the individual forces of Earth, Air, Fire, and Water as well as their combinations. Because most of the energies in the Minor Arcana are also present in the Major Arcana, Tarot Alchemy on the Major Arcana should reveal similar information as Tarot Alchemy on the Minor Arcana or the whole deck. Since there are 3003 binary combinations of the seventy-eight Tarot cards, and only 231 combinations using the Major Arcana, I decided to limit the scope of this book to the Major Arcana, thinking that the principles explained in the process will aid the reader in the analysis of readings utilizing the entire deck.

If you took the Pages out of the Minor Arcana, you would have today's fifty-two card deck of modern playing cards! It would be possible to do Tarot readings using ordinary playing cards, but without the Major Arcana, some detail and subtlety would be missing.

Some basic information about the Minor Arcana can be analyzed as follows:

- The Threes represent Saturn.
- The Fours represent Jupiter.
- The Fives represent Mars.

- The Sixes represent the Sun.
- The Sevens represent Venus.
- The Eights represent Mercury.
- The Nines represent the Moon.

The four suits correspond to the four elements. Wands = Fire, Cups = Water, Swords = Air and Pentacles = Earth.

For example the Six of Wands equals the Sun + Fire which points to Leo, which is the Strength card. Is this redundant? Not really. The Minor Arcana equals the outer world, and the Major Arcana equals the inner world. So even though the 6 of Wands and Strength cards are both (Sun + Fire) interactions, they are expressed in the external and internal worlds respectively.

The following Minor Arcana cards are directly linked to the Major Arcana through the Zodiac:

- Five of Wands equals Aries, which equals the Emperor.
- Seven of Pentacles equals Taurus, which equals the Hierophant.
- Eight of Swords equals Gemini, which equals the Lovers.
- Nine of Cups equals Cancer, which equals the Chariot.
- Six of Wands equals Leo, which equals Strength.
- Eight of Pentacles equals Virgo, which equals the Hermit.
- Seven of Swords equals Libra, which equals Justice.
- Five of Cups equals Scorpio, which equals Death.
- Four of Wands equals Sagittarius, which equals Temperance.
- Three of Pentacles equals Capricorn, which equals the Devil.
- Three of Swords equals Aquarius, which equals the Star.
- Four of Cups equals Pisces, which equals the Moon.

In general, the Minor Arcana cards represent external changes and events, while the Major Arcana cards represent internal or spiritual changes.

The numbered cards in the Minor Arcana (ace-ten) represent the Element-Planet interaction. The Court cards represent people, which are normally the subjects and objects of most questions posed by clients.

THE COURT CARDS

The sixteen Court cards are a subset of the Minor Arcana. They are the binary combinations of the four elements. The Court cards represent people and are the Element-Element interactions. The Court cards are the result of Alchemy on the four elements. There is no planet directly associated to them, but planets can be inferred indirectly. For example, by knowing that the King of Wands = Aries, Leo or Sagittarius, there is a link to the planets Mars, Sun and Jupiter indirectly through the Zodiac.

In the Tarot deck, The Kings are Fire, the Queens are Water, the Knights are Air, and the Pages are Earth. The Wands are fire, the Cups are Water, The Swords are Air and the Pentacles are Earth. In general, a King is an older man, while a Knight is a younger man. The Queen is an older woman while the Page is a younger woman. The Court cards represent the actors on the stage of life. By knowing who will intersect with you, how, why and were, you can understand how to take advantage of opportunity or avoid problems in life with more ease.

Here is some basic information about the Court cards.

Court Card	Rank	Suit	Planet	Energy
King of Wands	FIRE	FIRE	Mars, Sun, Jupiter	+
Queen of Wands	WATER	FIRE	Mars, Sun, Jupiter	−
Knight of Wands	AIR	FIRE	Mars, Sun, Jupiter	+
Page of Wands	EARTH	FIRE	Mars, Sun, Jupiter	−
King of Cups	FIRE	WATER	Jupiter, Moon, Mars	−
Queen of Cups	WATER	WATER	Jupiter, Moon, Mars	+
Knight of Cups	AIR	WATER	Jupiter, Moon, Mars	−
Page of Cups	EARTH	WATER	Jupiter, Moon, Mars	+
King of Swords	FIRE	AIR	Saturn, Mercury, Venus	+
Queen of Swords	WATER	AIR	Saturn, Mercury, Venus	−
Knight of Swords	AIR	AIR	Saturn, Mercury, Venus	+
Page of Swords	EARTH	AIR	Saturn, Mercury, Venus	−
King of Pentacles	FIRE	EARTH	Saturn, Venus, Mercury	−
Queen of Pentacles	WATER	EARTH	Saturn, Venus, Mercury	+
Knight of Pentacles	AIR	EARTH	Saturn, Venus, Mercury	−
Page of Pentacles	EARTH	EARTH	Saturn, Venus, Mercury	+

THE MAJOR ARCANA

The twenty-two cards of the Major Arcana give rise to 231 binary combinations. This is the subject of this book. In order to define the interactions between two Tarot cards, some basic information about the Tarot trump is necessary. The following table shows information about the Planet and Element associated with a Tarot card. This is the basic information needed for Tarot Alchemy. This is the "periodic table" of Tarot Alchemy.

#	Major Arcana Trump	Letter	Zodiac	Planet	Element	Day of Week
0	The Fool	I R			AIR	
1	The Magician	A J S		Mercury		Wednesday
2	The High Priestess	B K T		Moon		Monday
3	The Empress	C L U		Venus		Friday
4	The Emperor	D M V	Aries	Mars	FIRE	Tuesday
5	The Hierophant	E N W	Taurus	Venus	EARTH	Friday
6	The Lovers	F O X	Gemini	Mercury	AIR	Wednesday
7	The Chariot	G P Y	Cancer	Moon	WATER	Monday
8	Strength	H Q Z	Leo	Sun	FIRE	Sunday
9	The Hermit	I R	Virgo	Mercury	EARTH	Wednesday
10	The Wheel of Fortune	A J S		Jupiter		Thursday

11	Justice	B K T	Libra	Venus	AIR	Friday
12	The Hanged Man	C L U			WATER	
13	Death	D M V	Scorpio	Mars	WATER	Tuesday
14	Temperance	E N W	Sagittarius	Jupiter	FIRE	Thursday
15	The Devil	F O X	Capricorn	Saturn	EARTH	Saturday
16	The Tower	G P Y		Mars		Tuesday
17	The Star	H Q Z	Aquarius	Saturn	AIR	Saturday
18	The Moon	I R	Pisces	Jupiter	WATER	Thursday
19	The Sun	A J S		Sun		Sunday
20	Judgment	B K T			FIRE	
21	The World	C L U		Saturn		Saturday

The twenty-two cards of the Major Arcana represent the pathways between the spheres on the Tree of Life. The Major Arcana is the result of the Alchemy of Numerology. By examining where a Tarot trump appears on the Tree of life, the numbers that led to its creation can be revealed.

1-2 The Fool
1-3 The Magician
1-6 High Priestess
2-3 The Empress
2-6 The Emperor
2-4 The Hierophant
3-6 The Lovers
3-5 The Chariot
4-5 Strength
4-6 The Hermit
4-7 Wheel of Fortune

5-6 Justice
5-8 Hanged Man
6-7 Death
6-9 Temperance
6-8 The Devil
7-8 The Tower
7-9 The Star
7-1 The Moon
8-9 The Sun
8-1 Judgement
9-1 The World

Study the Tree of Life and the placement of the Major Arcana upon its paths and the above information will make more sense to you.

Here are some traditional meanings of the Major Arcana. Again, this is not the focus of this book. There are many books that give interpretations of the individual Tarot cards, and I suggest you seek out as many different opinions and interpretations as possible to define the cards internally for you. The focus of this book is the interactions and "spiritual reactions" that take place when the Tarot cards are combined in a reading. By understanding the exact question, the exact answer can be given. This should give you a starting point in your own analysis and interpretation of the Tarot cards. I have not included the meanings of the Minor Arcana as this is not the focus of this book. There are many excellent Tarot books out there that can give you descriptions of the individual cards in the Tarot deck.

The Fool (0): Carefree, foolish, extravagant, impetuous, indiscrete, and vague. The Fool is a child sampling life. Naive. Spontaneous. Endearing. Exploring where his whims take him. Anything is possible. But his little dog may be warning him not to step too close to the edge of the cliff. The Fool may be studying the stars when he should be looking where his next step will land. He may be a likely victim of trickery and deception. An easy target for bullying. Traditionally, also a suggestion of careless and excessive sexuality. This card more than any other represents the subject experiencing the influences of the diverse cast of characters in the Tarot deck. This is the Air element. The Fool card is silence, referencing the vacuum of space and the space between the words. Pure thought and ideas.

The Magician (1): Masculine, talented, creative, ingenious, proficient, gifted, and in control of the four elements. The Magician represents your will. He is Mercury. This card represents mathematics and logic. He is your ego. This is someone who is finally in control of the four elements and knows the secret to manifesting all his desires. He is a scientist or doctor and represents someone from the medical profession like a doctor or a nurse. We can create physical objects from raw materials using our mental and manual skills, and we can create and recreate ourselves continuously. It is a card of conscious awareness, concentration, and power. This is the card for someone who is committed and not afraid to act. Logic, mathematics and science. Communication and computers.

The High Priestess (2): Feminine, the unknown, secrets, mystery, and confident. The High Priestess points to the time period of the new moon. Surprising revelations may be coming. The High Priestess card represents illumination, knowledge, and truth. She is eminently feminine, mysterious, secretive, and intuitive. Moody and aloof. Knowing all but expressing her secrets by measure or through symbolism. Yet she is a powerful advisor. She is a well of knowledge, but only a cup at a time is dispensed. This card may often represent the subject (if female) or the object of the subject's desire (if male). Also, perhaps a suggestion for introspection or meditation. Traditionally, she represents knowledge, modesty, and discretion. Psychic energy and hidden mysteries.

The Empress (3): Feminine, motherly, fertility, creation, productive, fruitful, and grandmotherly. The Empress is Venus, goddess of love and beauty. Birth. Growth. Development. Nurturing. The Empress is a good mother. Fruitful, benevolent, loving, and caring. A person of station who is deserving of respect. When one is seeking answers, the card may indicate motherly worries about people or projects. It may raise the question of too much mothering or overprotectiveness. It may also be a reminder to the seeker that patience and persistence are necessary when he or she is nurturing growth. Traditionally, fertility, wealth, marriage, a female family member.

The Emperor (4): Masculine, fatherly, authority, stability, protective, advisor, military, government, and police. Aries rules the Emperor card. It is a man of war, represented by the planet Mars and Fire. It is a military figure who is very much in command. He represents authority figures, such as the police and government officials. This is someone who uses power to control his surroundings. It is a card of structure, authority, regulation, and the chain of command. It is a card of protection and defending. It is a card of being systematic and creating order. It is working within the framework of the legal system. It is a card of reorganization. Violent destruction.

The Hierophant (5): Marriage, union, relationships, celebration, consent, blessing, and approval. This card represents higher education and libraries. It is a card of college and classes. You will be involved in some social group and could be involved with someone from a university. You should attend classes. It is a card of following the rules and trying to fit in with the group. It is a sense of loyalty and belonging. It is the learning of culture and behavior by observance. You will be joining an organization, or you will experience some type of union. It is a sense of belonging to the group. It is joining a "club" or fraternity. This is card number five, so this number will be important. Taurus rules this card. It is organized religion. Art, music and nature.

The Lovers (6): Partners, lovers, union, combination, relationships, and attachment. I don't need to expound too much on this card. The meaning of this card is quite obvious. It represents a man and a woman coming together in a love relationship. This card affects people on many different levels, spiritual, physical, mental, and emotional. It represents your soul mate. The Zodiac sign of Gemini also rules the Lovers. It is a card of true love and marriage. It is a card of joy, fulfillment, and sensual pleasure. It is the ability to join the male and female aspects of your personality into one integrated whole. This card sometimes represents a choice between two lovers. Conscious decisions made in a relationship. Communication with a lover.

The Chariot (7): Transportation, movement, journey, relocation, change, and progress. The Chariot represents a vehicle or a car. Are you planning to buy or sell a car? It could also represent dealings with car insurance companies. It is ruled by Cancer, and its number is seven. (The seventh month is Cancer.) It represents changes occurring around you, even when you are at rest! It also represents the changing cycles of the Moon and the rotation of the lunar energies. You are determined to succeed. You are trying to focus your energies. You will rise above temptation. This card is self-confidence. You should have faith in yourself and look out for your interests. This is the ability to master your emotions and curb your impulses. Intuition. This is the ability to maintain discipline and hold in anger.

Strength (8): Fortitude, strength, power, energy, vitality, and force. Leo rules the Strength card. It is a card of spiritual strength. It is the control of your animalistic instincts and emotions and control of mind over matter. You will overcome your adversaries. It is also a card of physical strength, and it is very fortunate in questions about health. This is a card for someone who is patient and has stamina. This is someone who can maintain his or her composure even when angered. This is a card of compassion and empathy, the ability to understand how others are feeling. It is the ability to persuade or influence people to act as you wish. It is a card of inner and external strength. It is a card of courage and the need for reason to control emotion. Energy and healing.

The Hermit (9): Solitude, reflection, guidance, soul-searching, thinking, detachment, and wisdom. The Zodiac sign Virgo rules the Hermit card (number nine). It is someone who has been isolating themselves from others and who is searching within for answers. The number nine also refers to the Moon, so Mondays will be very strong days. Virgo is ruled by Mercury, so Wednesday will be a strong day as well. You will receive guidance from an older mentor. It is a time for introspection. Spend your time alone. Give or receive guidance. Concentrate and look for answers internally, not externally. This is someone who may withdraw from the world. It is a wise, bearded man. The month of September is indicated. Wisdom.

The Wheel of Fortune (10): Destiny, cycle of life, direction, future, change, opportunity, protection, Karma. The Wheel of Fortune represents Karma. It is the law of cause and effect. The forces are there, but balance and control is essential. This is a card of balance. All four elements are balanced. Earth, Air, Fire, and Water are in harmony, so the wheel spins. It represents the fluctuations of luck, both good and bad. It is a card of good fortune and gambling. It is a card of unexpected luck and good fortune, both financial and bodily health. Jupiter rules this card. The day of the week associated with Jupiter is Thursday. This card tells me that there may be events that are "out of your hands" happening because of the law of cause and effect. Constructive energy. Blessings and protection.

Justice (11): Legal, balance, equality, justice, law, court, judges, lawyers, and legal documents. Libra, the scales, rules the Justice card. This can give a clue as to when events might take places. It is the balance. It is Karma. It also means that you will have some dealings with the court system, and legal action and the advice of Lawyers will be needed. It also means that if you have been wronged, you will get your just reward, but if you have wronged others, you will be judged with equal harshness. This card is the judgment of Karma. You must endure events to keep the scales balanced. It can be harsh, but if others have wronged you, you will be rewarded. This card is ruled by Venus and Air, so you may be looking at your love relationship in an analytical or logical way. This is not an emotional card. The beauty of symmetry and balance.

The Hanged Man (12): Suspend, stopped, restricted, limited, discontinued, and ceased. This is a card of self-sacrifice, giving up the lesser good for the greater good. Just as the sun sacrifices its light for the benefit of the earth, so you will sacrifice for the greater good! It is a card of giving up personal pleasures for your own long-term benefit. It can represent someone who wants to quit smoking or even go on a diet. This is a very spiritual card, and its number is twelve. This number will somehow be significant and connected to your question. This is a card of doing something you don't want to do because deep down you know it is the right thing to do. Water.

Death (13): End, destruction, finish, cease, final, and loss. Scorpio rules the Death card. It can mean a physical death; however, it usually represents the end of one cycle and the beginning of another. The death card is number thirteen, and it refers to the thirteen full moons that exist every year. Hence, another reference to the element of water, to which Scorpio also belongs. For every death, there is a birth. It can also represent a funeral or burial service. It can also represent divorce. It is a final end. It is a transition. This card may signify an inevitable event, something that you must face no matter how hard you try to avoid it. Some aspect of your life is coming to a complete close. It is the spirit world and ghosts. Destructive emotions.

Temperance (14): Balance, restraint, control, alternative, and moderation. The Temperance card refers to the Zodiac sign of Sagittarius. It represents balance and equilibrium, and in questions of health, it refers to the circulatory and electrolytic systems of the body. It foretells of a time when the balance will be restored, and it is ruled by the planet Jupiter. It is a very fortunate card. The Temperance card is the ability to mix and balance opposite forces into a harmonious mixture. This is the card of the diplomat who can mix well in many different environments. The blessings of Jupiter and the fire and energy of Sagittarius are present. It is a card of prayer and communication with the angels. Constructive behaviors.

THE DEVIL.

The Devil (15): Anger, violence, jealousy, selfishness, resentment, animosity, temptation, and evil. This card represents Capricorn and the planet Saturn, which rules waiting periods, obstacles, and unexpected setbacks that will demand much of your attention. It is also a card of greed and bondage to the material world. It is a temptation to do something that you know is wrong. It is a warning. This is a card of confusion, addiction, and bad habits. This is a card of negative emotions and hatred. It is revenge and destructive actions masked as pleasure. It is self-deception. Things that are old. Watches and clocks.

THE TOWER.

The Tower (16): Destruction, breakdown, stress, downfall, loss, ruin, and unexpected change. The Tower is the energy of Mars. It is the lightning in the sky. It represents changes (and some can be violent) that will take place rapidly like the striking of lightning. It will change everything. It can be a warning about a dangerous situation or even a house fire. Be careful around fire or electricity. This is a card of sudden change, release, and revelation. Your plans may be suddenly disrupted. This is a card of emotional outbursts and uncontrolled emotional expression. It is a humbling experience or damage to the ego. It is also a card of sudden revelation, seeing the truth in a brilliant flash. A sudden revelation on your part may lead to an upheaval in your present life, which could lead to great change.

The Star (17): Prospects, hopes, opportunity, favorable, perspective, destiny, and time travel. This card represents the Zodiac sign of Aquarius. It is ruled by the planet Saturn, and sometimes it forewarns of a waiting period. It is a card of hope and inspiration in the future. The angel shown on the card has one foot in the water and one foot on the land. This channel is necessary to effect change in the world and to manifest your desires. It is sometimes a card of pessimism and self-doubt. This could represent a person with low self-esteem. It is also a card of memories and inspiration. Don't let pessimism destroy a possible renewal. Thoughts received from the future or past.

The Moon (18): Caution, beware, moody, deception, obscure, and risk. The Moon is ruled by the element of water. It is the subconscious mind, and it is ruled by the fluctuations of the Moon. Pay careful attention when there is a full moon or new moon. This will give you clues as to when action should be taken. Be patient and control your emotions. This is sometimes a card of fear and deception. It is a card of ghosts and spirits. Trust your instincts. The Moon is number eighteen, so this number will be significant. It is a card of deep self-realization. It is a journey of the soul into a place where there are no words, just images. It is a card of dreams and illusions, reflection and diffraction. Constructive emotions. Generosity.

THE SUN .

The Sun (19): Success, happiness, abundance, rewarding, productivity, and achievement. The Sun card is the attainment of all your goals and wishes. It is happiness. It is your youth. It is the highest collective human intellect. If you have been having health problems, this is a card of healing, and it also represents the daylight hours. This is a very strong card in questions of religion and spirituality. It is a card of enlightenment, greatness, vitality, and assurance. It is someone who has realized the truth and has had an intellectual breakthrough. It is someone who is the center of attention and who will set an outstanding example during a moment of personal glory. It is confidence and the ability to forgive. The light of the Sun illuminates the darkness, revealing the truth. Healing and enlightenment.

JUDGEMENT.

Judgement (20): Renewal, change, upheaval, transfer, alter, transformation, rebirth, and forgiveness. This card tells me that you have made a wrong judgment about someone. Either you trusted someone you shouldn't have, or you didn't trust someone you should have! There is a very important decision you must make, but you are hesitant to do so until you have all the facts. This is a card of baptism and purification. It is the use of the intellect without emotion. This is a card of forgiveness and the washing away of the sins of the past. The dead are rising from their coffins. It is a card of rebirth and renewal. Fire. Second chances.

The World (21): Assured, surety, positive, certainty, reward, success, and time travel. The World card is the last card of the deck, and it means that you will achieve your desires. You will be successful! Saturn rules it, however, so this is a card of earned success. There is a waiting period involved, and the number three tells me that Saturdays will be the time for action and decisions. It is a card of accomplishment, fulfillment, and involvement. It is the ability to bring all the components together to work in harmony. This is the ability to make your dreams come true. This is the card of someone who contributes to society. It is a healer. It is someone who renders a service. You should make use of your gifts and talents and share what you have. Give of yourself and be active. Now is the time to enjoy peace of mind. It is a time of contentment and satisfaction. Remember that in order to hold the world in your hands, you must give of yourself. Time. Eternity.

THEORY

As a professional Tarot reader, I have learned that the best way to see specifics in a Tarot reading is to analyze the combinations of the Tarot cards, not just the cards alone. For example, if the Tower card and Chariot card both show up in a Tarot reading, the individual card meanings will give information, but it is the combination of the two cards that gives detail and clarity. Of course, the interpretation of the interaction must be in harmony with the context of the question. Since the Tower card is negative and destructive and the Chariot card can represent a car, it can point to a possible car accident. Since the Tower represents Mars and the military, the combination can point to a military vehicle or tank. Looking at these two cards individually would not yield this type of detailed specific information.

Any Tarot card in the deck really has at least seventy seven different meanings. That is, itself combined with all of the other seventy seven cards of the deck. If the binary interactions of every Tarot card in the deck were described, it would lead to 3003 combinations! Since the Major Arcana is composed of twenty two cards, this leads to 231 combinations. This is reasonable and is the subject of this book. By learning the rules and details of these interactions, one should be able to extrapolate their abilities and understand the interactions of the entire deck.

Some Tarot cards may seem redundant at first. For example The 8 of Swords = Mercury + Air. This is Gemini. The Lovers Card is also Gemini, so does this mean that the 8 of Swords = The Lovers card? Not really, the Minor Arcana represents the mundane external world, while the Major Arcana represents the internal world. The energies of these two cards are similar, but their effects occur on different levels of reality. So, even though I have only included the 231 combinations of the Major Arcana, by understanding the patterns and details of the analysis, one should be able to interpret any two Tarot cards from the entire deck.

In a Tarot reading, of course individual card meanings are required, but it is the interactions of the cards with each other that give insight and detail in the reading. The individual Tarot cards represent the subjects and the objects and energies present, while the interaction shows the flow of the energy. Sometimes in a reading, a positive card and a negative card may both appear. How should this be handled? It is important to know which Tarot cards reinforce each other and which cancel each other out. Their proximity to each other in a spread also gives detail as to the strength of the interaction. Constructive and destructive interactions must be analyzed. For example, Fire cancels Water, and Earth cancels Air.

People have asked me, "How did you learn to read Tarot cards?" Experience and time. The answer is that the Tarot cards first taught me their language, and then I began to unravel their messages. Numbers are the language of the Tarot. By getting feedback from clients over the years, my interpretations of the Tarot cards and their combinations became calibrated with reality. By knowing which cards correspond to which person and the timing etc., clients often told me of the success and failures of my interpretations of the Tarot reading. When a client claimed that the Tarot cards were wrong, I noticed flaws in their original question that could lead to logical confusion. The exact wording of the original question is the most important part of the Tarot reading.

Questions to the Tarot cards should be direct and defined. There is no emotional guesswork in answering direct questions. If the interpretation of the cards and the answer to the question is objective then it is more likely to be correct. Although I feel that there is a time and a place for the use of purely intuitive energy, seeing visions and using the mind's eye to answer questions, I don't feel that the purely intuitive approach suits the Tarot cards. Some readers focus only on the pictures and forget the science behind the numerology and astrology symbols. They focus on how the cards make them feel. Numerology is the language of the Tarot cards, and it speaks loudly and clearly. If you have a defined question, a precise answer can be obtained. Be direct. A long, flowery question does not guarantee a wonderful spiritual experience from the Tarot. And sometimes a question can be answered in one word rather than some long, flowing prose about what all the influences might be. Just because the answer to a Tarot question is short does not mean it is not important. Some clients are surprised when they don't get a page-and-a-half, detailed analysis of their lives but are surprised when the exact question that they asked came true exactly as the Tarot revealed. Educating the person seeking guidance from the Tarot cards is helpful in revealing the future in a useful way. The question is the most important part of a Tarot reading.

How do Tarot cards work?

Most forms of divination follow the laws of synchronicity. Synchronicity is the experience of two or more events that are apparently unrelated or unlikely to occur together by chance but that are observed to occur together in a meaningful manner. The entire Tarot deck represents the entire universe. When the cards are shuffled and turned facedown, they represent the unknown universe. Because the question is posed at the moment the cards are drawn, the laws of synchronicity say that the Tarot cards will reveal the answer to the question or at least give added insight. Sometimes in order to answer a question, it is important to understand why it is being asked.

The understanding of synchronicity is essential to the study of Tarot Alchemy. The Tarot cards can be looked at as a mirror of reality and all of its potential. When a question is asked, and Tarot cards chosen, the symbols naturally reflect energies connected to the question in past present and future. By analyzing these symbols correctly and objectively, the truth about the question is revealed. Divination is the practical use of synchronicity to reveal hidden truth. The laws of attraction and sympathetic magic are all based on the principle of synchronicity.

There is no such thing as random. Even a computer cannot generate a truly random number. A computer uses a complicated mathematical equation to generate a number that appears random but is based on a set of defined rules. There is no such thing as random. Everything has a cause and effect. Chaos theory teaches us that even complicated confusing patterns will have an underlying simple mechanism. It may appear random and complicated to the observer, but the initial causes are simple and beautiful.

Manifestation is an exothermic reaction. It gives off energy. When a thought becomes matter, then energy in the form of entropy or disorder is released. This energy is dispersed through time, so depending on frequency (repetition) and intensity (focus) of a thought, this will determine when manifestation will occur.

When two different energies of the Major Arcana are combined, the resulting manifestation releases more energy in the form of light and heat than the individual cards themselves. Understanding this concept is the key to controlling this particular energy and therefore seeing the spiritual light that is emitted.

The energy that is released when a thought becomes matter is distributed through time and space. There is an intellectual, emotional, behavioral and spiritual response to manifestation.

The laws of nature and biology reflect the same spiritual chemistry. The Tarot describes the interactions of various spiritual energies. The Major Arcana represent spiritual elements, and their reactions define reality. There are only four bases in DNA (the four elements), and it is the sequence of these energies that gives rise to structure and function in proteins. Because the Major Arcana represents the elemental and planetary forces, scientific analysis of the combination can also be made by inspection. Biochemistry and life itself is a reflection of spiritual truth.

Computers are the result of Tarot energies. The binary language of computers is a reflection of the dualistic nature of the universe. Study the I Ching to know more about this topic. With the swift communication that takes place today, Tarot creates a new form of psychic energy that can travel through computer networks. E-mail and telephone readings remain valid and are a very useful way to get a Tarot reading. It is not necessary for a client to physically be present with the Tarot to receive the message.

PRACTICE

What is divination? Divination is defined as the art or practice that seeks to foresee or foretell future events or discover hidden knowledge usually by the interpretation of omens or by the aid of supernatural powers. The Tarot cards can be used in many ways. They can be used in meditation, as a Talisman or as a tool of divination. The Tarot can be used as an oracle, to answer questions, or give insight. They can be used to see the past, present or future. The Tarot can be used to view situations from new perspectives. If used properly, the Tarot cards can be used to answer any question conceivable.

A Tarot spread is a specific layout of the Tarot cards. Each position of the card represents a different aspect. These kinds of readings normally don't look at card combinations, but they look at the meaning of the card in context with the aspect that the position in the spread represents. Tarot Alchemy can be used on positional spreads, but the information may be confusing or conflicted due to the nature of the positional meanings. A more precise way to approach a Tarot reading is to answer questions one at a time. Three cards are chosen. The first card revealed represents the past, the next one is the present and the third one is the future. The sequence that the cards are chosen gives a general timeline and shows the sequence of events and energy flow.

Because the twenty-two Tarot cards of the Major Arcana are broken down into the twelve Zodiac cards, seven planetary cards, and three of the four elements, an analysis can be scientifically done. Using numerology, astrology, Kabbalah, and traditional meanings with Tarot

Alchemy, a complete analysis of the Tarot cards can be done. By using the laws of numerology, Kabbalah, and astrology, detailed explanations can be revealed in the combinations.

So why even get a Tarot reading?

The purpose of a Tarot reading is to analyze a situation from a new or unknown perspective. It is possible to change the future in this way. By learning about potential problems before they arise, you can sidestep the negativity that is on the way. By seeing hidden opportunity, positive and productive actions can be taken.

Sometimes it is good to step out of a situation and look at the situation from a new perspective. The most important part of a Tarot reading is the question.

The ability to understand a Tarot reading increases the more you attempt to do so. Experiment with the cards. Play with them. Ask them to reveal their nature to you. A muscle gets stronger the more you use it, so use the Tarot cards every day. A chemist experiments with chemicals and elements in a laboratory. The Magician uses Tarot Alchemy to create spiritual reactions and understands the messages that the interactions are trying to convey. Ultimately, the combination of the elements creates new and more specific forms of energy that can shape the future. The ability to understand the combinations of the Tarot cards leads to true insight in the analysis of a Tarot reading.

The combinations of the Tarot cards in a Tarot spread and their arrangements define the flow of energy. Are there blockages to this flow? For example in the combination Moon, Emperor, Chariot, notice that the flow of the cards is WATER FIRE WATER. Since fire is in the midst of so much water, the fiery nature of the Emperor card is cancelled out by the Water. In addition, the Waters are separated from each other by Fire and their connection is weaker. Compare this to Moon, Chariot, Emperor, where the energy flow is WATER WATER FIRE. The two Water signs are side by side and therefore strengthened. This Water can overcome the Fire of the Emperor.

Can my consultation of the Tarot cards change the future? Yes, as a matter of fact, the whole purpose of a Tarot reading is to enable someone to shape the future the way they desire by making the right set of choices along their path. One mistake on the decision making process can lead to setbacks in the manifestation process. Most people suffer because they don't really know exactly what they truly want! How can you manifest something if you don't know what it is? How can you manifest something if you are not sure you truly want it? Once a question is defined, Tarot cards chosen and Tarot Alchemy applied; there is no limit as to what can be manifested.

What is the purpose of a Tarot reading? I use Tarot to answer specific questions. The Tarot can give new insight and perspectives on situations, people, and relationships. Once you understand the language of the Tarot cards, they can tell you many things! The Tarot cards can help you avoid pitfalls and take advantage of opportunities.

It is essential to have a basic understanding of the four elements and seven planets in order to analyze the interactions. Many of the terms mentioned here come from Tarot card combinations described by Dorothy Kelly, paraphrased from one of her excellent books. She used key words and gave many examples of two-, three-, and four-card combinations. She spent a lot of time distinguishing between upright and inverted cards. In my opinion, an inverted Tarot card in a spread usually indicates a situation or energy with latent or dormant potential. An inverted card can represent a weaker potential, but the energy is still similar, not a complete polar opposite. In my treatment of the card combinations, I am looking at the pure elemental and planetary forces. Intuition is needed to know when an inverted Tarot card points to latent potential or just weaker energy.

Kelly also spends a lot of time distinguishing which Tarot card comes first. She makes a difference between "the Magician and the Moon" order and "the Moon and the Magician" order. In my analysis of the combinations, I describe the nature of the energy flow from both directions. Generally, in a three-card reading, the sequence in which the cards are revealed gives clues to the time line. It is past, present future. All the interactions should be looked at and given equal weight. The flow of energy from one card to the next must also be examined for a clearer picture of the situation and results. It is important to note which Tarot cards are inverted and in what sequence the cards are revealed. Only then the thermodynamics of the Tarot spread can be analyzed accurately and precisely.

That is how divination works. The symbols expressed in the Tarot cards directly mirror reality in time and space. A well-phrased question with proper objective analysis leads to truth beyond what can be seen without the use of the Tarot cards.

I have chosen to use the Tarot cards as an oracle—that is, to answer specific questions at certain times. In my experience, this is the most efficient, accurate, and precise method of using the Tarot cards. It is all based on numerology, the four elements, the seven planets, and the Tarot Alchemy between them all. By defining the question, a defined answer is easily obtained. One question is asked, and three cards are drawn.

Usually, the order in which the cards are revealed represents a general flow of energy from past, present, and future. All of the combinations of the Tarot cards are examined, and the results revealed based on logical rules of which elements and planets are expressed in the reading. All of the combinations should be given equal weight. The three card reading is also useful because it represents the interaction between will, force and form. For example the form could be a car. The force is the fuel. The will is represented by the driver of the car. When analyzing a three card Tarot reading, try to identify which Tarot cards are connected to the form, the force and the will. This will aid in the analysis of a Tarot reading. It is also important to focus on the exact question that is asked. An analysis of the exact nature of the question will reveal an exact answer. Secrets can be revealed.

When you are consulting the Tarot cards, make sure that you specify what you want to know. Do you want to know what day of the week or the month you should have an appointment? Both of these questions can be answered specifically, but the question must be defined prior to consulting the Tarot cards. These questions are similar but distinctively different as well. Do not try to answer a question that was not asked.

Sometimes the Tarot cards can give additional information, but for clarity, focus only on one question at a time. This method is very accurate and precise and has never let me down.

I thought it might be interesting to try to arrange the Major Arcana in one big circle, using all twenty-two Tarot cards linked to each other through element, planet or numerology. Each card must be linked to its neighbor by planet, element or numerology. After some trial and error, I found a few combinations that worked! I have never seen this type of cyclic arrangement where all of the Tarot cards are in harmony with its neighbor, but here is one example:

The Fool card is Air and is linked to Justice (also Air).

The Justice card is then linked to the High Priestess through numerology (11=2)

The High Priestess is then linked to the Moon card because the High Priestess equals the Moon.

The Moon card is then linked to the Wheel of Fortune. Both share the planet Jupiter, because the Moon card is ruled by Pisces (Jupiter and Water).

The Wheel of Fortune is then linked to the Sun card through numerology. The Sun card equals nineteen, which equals ten, which points to the Wheel of Fortune.

The Sun card is then linked to the Magician through numerology. Nineteen equals ten, which equals one. The Sun and the Magician are linked.

The Magician is then linked to the Hermit. Both share planet Mercury.

The Hermit is then linked to the Hierophant. Both share the Earth element.

The Hierophant is then linked to the Empress. Both share the planet Venus.

The Empress is then linked to the World through numerology. The Empress equals three, which equals twenty-one and represents the World.

The World is then linked to the Hanged Man through numerology. (21=12)

The Hanged Man is linked to the Chariot. Both share the Water element.

The Chariot is then linked to the Tower through numerology. (7=16)

The Tower is then linked to the Death card. Both share the planet Mars.

The Death card is then linked to Temperance. Death equals thirteen, which equals four and represents Jupiter. Temperance equals Jupiter, too. Temperance equals fourteen, which equals five and represents Mars. The Death card is Mars.

The Temperance card is then linked to the Emperor. Both share the Fire element.

The Emperor is the linked to Judgement. They share the Fire element.

The Judgement card is then linked to Strength. They share the Fire element.

The Strength card is then linked to the Lovers. The Strength card equals the Sun, which in turn equals six and represents the Lovers. The Lovers card is Gemini, which equals Mercury and eight, the Strength Card.

The Lovers is then linked to the Devil card through numerology. The Lovers equals six, which equals fifteen and represents the Devil.

The Devil is then linked to the Star. They share the planet Saturn.

The Star is then linked back to the starting point, the Fool, through the element of Air.

I have found a few different "circles" of Major Arcana that work out, and when you arrange them in such a way, you can feel the circle of energy grow! Arranging the Tarot cards in these cyclic arrangements is also a good way of studying the correspondences of the Tarot cards.

ANALYZING THE QUESTION

One of the most important parts of a Tarot reading, especially when the Tarot cards are being used as an oracle, is to define the question. If the question is general, then the answer should be general. If the question is specific, then the answer should be specific.

One mistake clients or readers make when analyzing a Tarot reading is trying to answer a question that was not asked, or giving too much information that may or may not be relevant. For clarity, I suggest that each question deserves its own Tarot spread. This is one reason I prefer to use a three card Tarot spread. It is perfectly designed for answering one specific question at a time.

The exact phrasing of the original question is important in a Tarot card consultation. It is not wise to ask "if-then" type questions as this can lead to ambiguous results. Questions should be logical, precise and seek only one piece of information at a time for clarity. There is a difference between asking "would I" or "should I" or "can I". It is best not to ask a question that can lead to an ambiguous answer. Yes / No questions are good for Tarot as well, although sometimes a 'maybe' might be the result.

I have been a professional Tarot reader for more than twenty years, so I have noticed some patterns to the types of questions that clients are interested in. Most questions asked of the Tarot cards involve other people. There are sixteen "people" cards (Court cards) in the Tarot deck. Half are male, and the other half are female. Half are young, and half are old. All the Zodiac signs and Elements are expressed. The percentage of

Court cards in the Tarot deck is about 20 percent or one out of five. This confirms the principle that people are the ones interacting with the four elements. The four elements along with spirit equal reality. Reality only exists through perception. When we are asking questions about other people, it is useful to know their first names and Zodiac signs if possible to reveal the message from the Tarot cards efficiently.

It is important to realize that the question is the most important part of a Tarot reading. If a question is specific, then the answer should be specific also. If you ask a general question like, "Will I have a happy life?" general energies and trends should be noticed in the cards. You can also ask a question like, "What color socks should I wear next Tuesday?" and the Tarot cards will tell you! Once the question is defined, it can be answered objectively by using numerology and Tarot Alchemy. Remove the twenty-two Tarot cards of the Major Arcana from the deck, shuffle them any way you want, and spread them out on the table in front of you. The way the cards are shuffled doesn't matter. You don't have to use only your left hand. These are all just ritual behaviors. There is benefit to doing things the same way every time, but to analyze a Tarot reading, this is not so important. Nothing else is needed. No candles. No crystals. No bowls of waters or bat wings. The only thing that is needed is the question. Some people feel that prayers, candles, or other rituals will benefit a Tarot reading, but in my experience, the most important aspect of a reading is the question. Rituals may help to build up an emotional connection in a Tarot reading, but as long as the Tarot cards are drawn in a random way, then the answers will be valid. Some people feel that a Tarot reading is not valid if a computer choses the cards. I disagree with this. A computer choosing the Tarot cards (as long as it is random) is just as valid as long as the question is clearly defined and connected to that drawing of the cards. I have a scientific opinion on this point. I use a computer program and my trusty, worn deck of Rider-Waite Tarot cards to choose cards, and the results I get are just as valid in either case. It is just that I have more of an emotional attachment to my physical deck than my virtual Tarot deck. In my experience, the client and reader will build in rituals automatically through normal use. People will fall into a pattern when they are experimenting, and this will lead to the development of ritual actions that will strengthen the Tarot reading. Spend time in understanding your question. Write it down and verbalize it. Be sure that it is not a conditional question. Remember, if you ask a general question, you will get a general answer. Ask for only one piece of information at a time. For example, don't ask, "What will be the first name and the Zodiac sign of my next wife?" In a three-card reading, it is possible to get this answer, but for clarity, every question deserves its own Tarot reading. It is not that much more work to ask one question, reshuffle, and repeat the process with a new question.

Sometimes I like to play a game called "Speed Tarot." I will write down a list of seven or eight specific questions (that does not mean long) and then shuffle the cards and then choose three Tarot cards and write them down. I put the cards back in the deck, reshuffle, choose three more, and continue the process until I have three cards for each question. After this, I will go back and analyze the cards that came up for each question and answer each corresponding question. By using this technique, an objective picture of the situation can be determined, and appropriate actions can be taken.

E-mail is an excellent way of communicating with clients and formulating proper questions for the Tarot cards. It forces the client to manifest their question in a detailed form and also creates a record of the question, the Tarot cards chosen, the interpretation and eventually the real world results. This information is valuable as it helps to calibrate the Tarot cards and the analysis to reality.

The most popular question asked by my clients concerns their relationships with other people. How do these other people feel? Why did they do what they did? Who will be there in the future? When will he contact me? The most common question is about relationships. Most questions involve the interactions between people. There is a parallel between the interactions of the Tarot cards and the interactions between people and situations. There is Alchemy between people as well. Tarot Alchemy can be used to determine the energy between two people by comparing the Zodiac signs and examining the Alchemy between their Zodiac signs. An understanding of what energies are present and when changes will occur can help you make decisions that will lead you to a positive future. Although the Tarot cards can tell you how to accomplish something or how to obtain something, there is no guarantee that doing so will be to your benefit. The old adage "Be careful what you wish for because you just might get it" applies here.

The same question should never be asked twice. This can lead to confusion. You shouldn't just sit there and keep asking the same question over and over until you choose the cards that you like! It is okay to get updates from the cards on a topic from time to time, but the Tarot cards must be respected if they are to work for you properly. Have faith in the Tarot cards.

Who? What? When? Where? Why? Which? Should I? Would I? Can I? These are all different types of questions and should be defined prior to consulting the Tarot cards.

When one is asking a "who" question, numerology can be used to find out first names. Zodiac signs can also be shown. Be careful with the word "who". It can be ambiguous. Be careful how you word your question. If you want to know the first letter of the person's first name, then ask for it. If you want to know the person's zodiac sign, then ask for it. For example, if you ask the question, "What is the first name of the person I should hire for the open position, Thomas, Daniel, or Michael?" If the three Major Arcana chosen are the Hanged Man (12), the Sun (19), and Death (13), using numerology, it is clear that the Death card, which equals 13 and represent M, references Michael. Clearly, Michael is the best choice. However, if you asked the question, "What Zodiac sign will the person be?" then the Death card points to Scorpio, and that would be the answer. Of course, it is necessary to know what Zodiac signs the three men are!

So you see, the specific way the exact question is worded has a direct result on the answer! This is a very important point to understand when one is consulting the Tarot cards. Garbage in, garbage out.

Usually, a "what" question turns out to be general or unpredictable. It is a question of action and verbs. What will happen? What will be the result? What object is needed? What actions need to be taken in order to accomplish something? Again, the wording of the question is important in the analysis of the answer. For example, a person could ask, "What should I spend my money on? Buying a new car or paying off debt?" If the three Major Arcana are the Wheel of Fortune (10), the Chariot (7), and the Sun (19), the appearance of the Chariot combined with the optimistic attitude of the Sun would indicate that buying a new car is the correct course of action. Again, examine the exact question before you try to answer a "what" question.

A "when" question is well suited to the Tarot cards. This is the most common question that people ask. When will they get what they want?! Again, be specific when you are asking a "when" question. For example, you may ask, "In what Zodiac sign will an event take place?" Or you could ask, "In what zodiac sign will I be offered a new job?" Or, "In what zodiac sign should I get married?" Because the Major Arcana is full of Zodiac cards, this question is answered directly and objectively. Many times, multiple time points can be indicated, so the result will come from decisions and actions taken. You may also ask, "On what day of the week" or "On what day of the month should I take action?" and the Tarot Cards can tell you directly. By using Tarot Alchemy, detailed information can be obtained, and effective actions can be taken. You can use the Tarot cards to help you determine when to play offense and when to play defense. Remember, there is a difference between asking "on what day of the week" and "in what month or year" something will occur. Each of these questions is distinct and deserves its own Tarot reading. Days of the month can also be determined using numerology. One general rule about when to play offense and defense is to follow the cycles of the moon. When the moon is waxing, this is generally a more positive time period, so it is beneficial to make changes and make decisions then. The waning moon generally indicates a negative time period, so it may be best to make decisions at a later time. It may be time to withdraw and spend time reflecting on one's internal development.

Cities, States, and Countries can also be determined by numerology. Perhaps a client wants to know if she should move to Ohio or Kentucky. If the three Major Arcana were the Devil (15), the Star (17), and the Moon (18), then the answer would be Ohio, because the Devil card = 15 = O = Ohio. When one is determining names of people or places, the first letter of the first name is usually the most influential. You can analyze your own first name by using numerology. Because my name is Ken, K is the most important letter in my name. K equals eleven, which represents the Justice card. The energy of Libra will be important in my life. Balance, music, and art are indicated. Venus and Air point to the logical or scientific aspect of art, music, or love. This book is an artistic expression of creative energy through the balance of logic. It is the synergistic result of the individual energies of each letter of each word. The 'whole' is more than the sum of its parts.

"Why" questions are about motivation. What emotions are present in the Tarot combinations? In a three-card reading, there are three different two-card combinations. Look them up in the paragraphs provided, and you should have your answer. Do not try to see the whole picture in one Tarot reading. Ask different questions from different perspectives to gain a true picture of what energies are at play and what the results are most likely to be. Adjusting your own behaviors through understanding can help you manifest your desires quicker. Go with the flow and know when to recharge your battery. Perhaps a client asked the question, "Why does my husband want a divorce?" and the Tarot cards were the Devil (15), the Tower (16), and the Hanged Man (12). The Devil card combined with the Tower points to anger and impulsive behavior. The combination of the Devil and the Hanged Man indicates a passive person who is emotionally lazy. The Hanged Man and The Tower combination points to an unpredictable person. He has anger issues and cannot conquer temptations and addictions that are affecting his behavior and stunting his emotional growth. Overall, a negative combination! It seems that her husband has many negative emotional problems and is selfish. He wants the divorce out of anger, addiction and lust.

Again, the exact wording of the question is necessary to answer a "how" question, too. "How can I make or help Nancy love me?" and "How can I find a lost key?" are completely different questions, so even if the exact three Tarot cards appeared for these questions, different aspects of the combinations would be emphasized in order to answer the question. The energy combinations need to be examined in context with the exact phrasing of the original question asked. If the Magician, the Chariot, and the Empress show up for the question about Nancy, the Magician card will point to communication. The Chariot equals travel, and the Empress points to nature. So inviting her to do some travel and watch the leaves change color would touch a spot in her heart and make her love you. Or perhaps the Chariot card says that the lost key was dropped in the car and perhaps picked up by the Empress (your mother). So a bit of intuition and a detailed analysis of the exact question is necessary to use the Tarot cards properly. By using this technique, any question can be answered exactly, precisely, accurately, and objectively. This is a very powerful source of information. After all, it comes as the result of Tarot Alchemy, and the light that it creates will be seen and experienced by you.

METHODOLOGY

In my experience a simple way to consult the Tarot cards with an accurate result is to ask one specific question, choose three Tarot cards and answer that question and that question alone. Rinse and repeat!

How can a Tarot reading be done? In order to use the Tarot efficiently, one specific question at a time should be asked. It is good to verbalize or even write the question down in order to manifest it in physical or verbal form. E-mails are good for this purpose as well. I have had good success doing Tarot reading through e-mail. After the question is formulated and manifested, three Tarot cards from the Major Arcana are drawn. You can keep drawing Tarot cards from the full deck until three Major Arcana appear. If it happens soon, say within six or seven cards, the answer to the question will reveal itself sooner. If it takes forty or fifty cards, then it may take years for the answer to the question to emerge. You can also separate the deck and only use the twenty-two cards of the Major Arcana.

Each Tarot Cards is broken down into a combination of one of the four elements and one of the seven planets. By deconstructing both Tarot cards into the elements and analyzing their interactions, a new "meaning" or blended analysis is created, which usually gives more detail and insight in a reading.

Steps for Analysis:

1. Examine the question so we know what to look for. Make sure that the question is well defined and includes basic information like first names and specifics.

2. Choose three cards from the Major Arcana.

3. What are the planets? Examine which planets are present in the three Tarot cards. Also, look at the combinations of the planets. Notice which planets are not present. Sometimes this can give information too.

4. What are the elements? Which elements are present? What order were they revealed in? Do they strengthen or weaken each other? Examine the combinations of the elements and what they mean.

5. Examine the numerology of the Tarot cards in the reading. Convert numbers into letters. Does this information relate to the original question?

6. Know the traditional Major Arcana card meanings. I have included some in this book, but this is not the focus of the book. I suggest you seek many other sources to get a whole picture of their traditional meanings. Examine the simple meaning of the Major Arcana as well.

7. Examine the analysis that I have provided. In a three-card Tarot reading, there are three combinations that should be examined.

8. Do these Tarot cards completely cancel each other out? Do they strengthen each other?

9. Are they active or passive? In general, Water and Earth are passive. Fire and Air are active. The combinations show various degrees of active and passive, and sometimes they cancel each other out. Odd numbers are active and even numbers are passive.

10. What is the sequence of the Tarot cards chosen? Are any of the cards inverted? Identify events from past, present to future. Identity Form, Form and Will.

11. The thermodynamics of a Tarot reading should be analyzed as well. The energy flow is important to understand. The energy flow of everyday events is also important to understand so that mirrors to these events can be defined and described by the card combinations.

12. Synthesize all of this information in a common sense way (and yes, perhaps with a small touch of intuition) and answer the question! Record the question, cards chosen and eventually the results.

Choose three Tarot cards from the Major Arcana. Anyway you decide to do it is okay, but you should stick with the same method time and time again to strengthen the interaction and your intuitive abilities to understand the message. Answer the original question and the original question only using the planets, elements, numerology, and combinations and interactions based on objective scientific rules. Insight and knowledge is then gained, and proper actions can be taken. Sometimes looking at what Tarot cards, planets or elements are not present in a Tarot reading can give insight into the answer to the question.

It is important to define the structure of the Tarot reading or Tarot spread before consulting the Tarot cards. It is important to know how many cards will be drawn. Will inverted cards be analyzed? It is essential to note what sequence the cards are drawn, what spread is used, the proximity of cards to each other and what their interactions are.

It is also good to find a Tarot spread that you are comfortable with and stick with it. Do it the same way every time. Practice and repetition builds up pathways in the brain and strengthens the analysis. There is value in doing things the same way every time. This is the basis of ritual magic and the power of repetition. Practice makes perfect. It is ok to know a variety of Tarot spreads, like the Pyramid or Tree of

Life, but in the end it is best to find the one that works best for you and stick with it. Rituals behavior is like a muscle, the more you use it, the stronger it gets.

I like the three card reading because it corresponds with proton, neutron and electron and past, present, and future. It is brief enough to answer one specific question with enough detail to give good advice to the client. The future is always in the hands of the client and their decisions will determine their fate, but when they come to the crossroads, the Tarot cards can give them a peek down each path. The Tarot cards can help you make better decisions and help you to analyze your own life from new and unexpected perspectives. The Tarot cards must answer any question you can think of because of the laws of synchronicity.

Some of my clients prefer me to shuffle my Tarot cards and choose three cards, as they do not trust a computer-generated Tarot reading. Is there a difference between computer-drawn Tarot readings and face-to-face or hand-drawn ones? No, as long as the cards are drawn randomly. This doesn't make sense to me, because in both cases, the choosing of the cards is completely random (or as close to random as possible!) It doesn't matter how the Tarot cards are chosen as long as it is randomly done. The important point is that the question should be well defined prior to choosing the Tarot cards. By choosing three Major Arcana cards and basing interpretations on the principles of Tarot Alchemy, the specific answer is accurately given.

Of course, there is no such thing as random. Even the throw of dice in a casino is not random. The cubes are subject to the laws of gravity and momentum and their result is in direct proportion to the energies put on them. The results may seem random, but there are underlying physics that describes the exact trajectories etc. The results on a craps table are not random. Even a slot machine is subject to the randomize function in a computer chip which is based on a complicated equation. Although it seems random on the surface, the underlying cause is not. This demonstrates the law of synchronicity.

When three Tarot cards are drawn, there are three "interactions" that should be examined. By combining two cards in three different ways, three "energy pathways" are revealed. By understanding the individual cards and the reactions among them, a complete picture of what will occur is revealed. The Tarot cards and the interactions between them are used to answer the question in a reading.

I use the Tarot cards as an oracle. That is, I use them to answer questions. I normally don't consult the Tarot cards without a question unless I am using a spread. A simple approach that works well is to write down the question. E-mail readings are good because they force the client to specify a question. Manifesting the question is important and necessary in order to manifest the answer to that question. Break the question down into its parts. Is it a "who", "what", "when", or "where" question? Once the question is defined, then the Tarot cards should be consulted. An analysis of the question is critical when one is trying to answer it! Do not answer a question that is not asked.

My website is sunmoontarot.com I do many e-mail readings. Any feedback from clients when they feel the Tarot reading is wrong is usually resolved when the original question is examined closely. A client may be searching for the answer to a question that was not originally asked. For clarity, one question at a time should be asked. Each question deserves its own Tarot reading. The Tarot cards are never wrong. Sometimes the interpretation can be off, but the message from the cards is always valid.

Some people have asked me, "How can you do a Tarot reading by e-mail? How can that work when the person is not face-to-face with you?" Although there is benefit to having the client physically present to select their own Tarot cards, it is not necessary. The most important part of the Tarot reading is the question. Because the question is sometimes e-mailed or written down, it is well defined, and the answer can be well defined. As long as the Tarot cards are chosen randomly, it doesn't matter who chooses them or how they are chosen.

I have been a professional Tarot reader for over twenty years. I don't normally use Tarot spreads. The most important part of a Tarot reading is the question. Once the question is defined, three Tarot cards are chosen. Before I give my answer, I look at each card and determine its elemental and planetary composition. For example, knowing that the Lovers card is Gemini (Mercury and Air) and the Four of Pentacles is Jupiter and Earth tells me that Air and Earth (thought and matter or objects) are related. The combination of Mercury and Jupiter points to constructive logic. So this combination points to physical things that are built or measured. Physical objects that evoke thought. This combination is a like married couple building a house. Communication is the outward expression of thought. This combination can represent an architect or engineer. It is someone who takes ideas into the manifestation phase constructively and logically. A successful result! On a symbolic level, the Lovers plus the Four of Pentacles can points to two lovers who move into a house together or buy a house. So you can see the usefulness of this technique of analysis. Because using the entire deck would give rise to 3,003 combinations, I have decided to limit this book to the Major Arcana (twenty-two cards), thinking that these definitions could help you in your interpretation of the rest of the Tarot deck as well.

TIME AND TIMING

Time and timing are important to consider in a Tarot reading. Karma is not instant. When you do something bad, you are not immediately punished. When you do something good, you are not immediately rewarded either! The Tarot cards can tell you when things will happen, or when the best times for you to take action will be. The amounts of punishment and reward are not exactly equal to the original deeds either! Because Karma, both good and bad, is dispersed through time and space, it is sometimes difficult to see the cause and effect behind this concept. The Tarot cards can help with understanding the flow of Karma (a form of energy) as well.

There are lots of ways to determine when something will happen using the Tarot cards. It depends on how the question is phrased. For example, there is a difference between asking "What year will I get married?" or "What day of the week should I schedule my appointment?" Once the question is defined, then the Tarot cards can answer. Numerology can be used to determine months and dates. For example, the six of Pentacles points to the sixth month, June. The Strength card is number eight and points to August. The 2 of Pentacles = February or November. In numerology 2 = 11, so the 2 of Pentacles can point to February or November.

If you ask "in what year will something occur?" you can use numerology to figure out the year. For example, if the three Tarot cards were The Moon (18), The Sun (19) and The Lovers (6). Then using numerology the choices for years would be: 2016, 2017, or 2013. If you ask "in what month will something occur?" you can use numerology for this as well.

For example the Chariot = 7 = July, or the Wheel of Fortune = 10 − October. You can also ask "during what Zodiac sign will something occur?", and then the Hermit would point to Virgo as the active time period.

For example, you may ask, "On what day of the week should I schedule my job interview?" The three Major Arcana drawn are the Hermit, the Lovers, and Judgement.

Because the Hermit = Virgo = Mercury, and the Lovers = Gemini = Mercury and the Judgment card is Fire, the answer to the question is Wednesday, Wednesday being the day of Mercury.

If the question is "What day of the month should I schedule my job interview?" and the Tarot cards were the Star (17), the Magician (1), and the Hanged Man (12), the answer would be the seventeenth, the first, or the twelfth of the month.

Asking the same question in multiple ways will give you an even more exact answer. You can use numerology to find the day of the month or the time of the day that will work for you. In regards to "when" questions, what if I ask "What time on Wednesday should I schedule my appointment?" The cards drawn are the Empress (3), the Moon (18), and the Hermit (9). The possible times would be three, nine, or six o'clock (eighteen). Perhaps 9:00 a.m. is the proper answer. Timing is easy to reveal if you ask for it properly in the question. Numerology reveals months, years and days of the month, while the Planetary forces reveal days of the week in a Tarot spread. However, these details must be asked for in the original question to be truly valid.

SOME THINGS TO THINK ABOUT

Here is a collection of random thoughts. I hope it helps in the analysis of your own Tarot readings and gives you some things to think about.

0   Who am I? My name is Kenneth. I am a Capricorn, and I have been a Tarot reader for over thirty years. I am a chemist and mathematician. Who are you? Which Court card represents you?

1   What do I want? I want to explain the interactions and reactions of all the combinations of Tarot cards in the Major Arcana. Eventually, I would like to do the entire deck. 3003 paragraphs! What do you want?

2   How do I feel? I feel content. I feel the need to manifest this information in physical form to effect positive change in the lives of others. How do you feel?

3   What will come from this effort? Tarot Alchemy will lead to an understanding of the linkage between inner and outer selves. The connection between the spiritual and material world will be revealed. An understanding of the interactions observed in the material world will be gained. Reality is the outer reflection of the inner spiritual truth. What are you searching for?

4   Can Planetary and Elemental energies be controlled? Knowledge is the first step in gaining control of a particular type of

energy. Without complete knowledge of Fire, can it truly be understood?

5   Can Interactions of the Tarot cards be understood? Why even do a Tarot reading? Difficult problems may be solved easier when viewed from new perspectives. Tarot readings can help you to solve problems and take advantage of opportunities. The Tarot cards can help you avoid pitfalls. Patterns that reinforce each other manifest faster. Sometimes energies cancel each other out.

6   Can energies be combined? Yes, however, there may be a variance in the time it takes to manifest based on the + / -nature of the interaction. A fortunate combination (for example fire + air) will manifest sooner than a negative interaction such as Air + Water or Earth + Fire.

7   Does energy move? Where will it go? Is the element active or passive? An active element usually manifests sooner rather than later. Fire and Air are active elements and Water and Earth are passive. What is your element?

8   How strong is an interaction? How near are two Tarot cards in a spread? Is the Fire fueled by Air? Is the Water controlled or dammed up by Earth?

9   What is the structure? The structure of the Tarot reveals the structure of reality. Twelve signs of Zodiac. Seven planets. Three of the four elements. (Why is the fourth element, Earth, missing in the Major Arcana?) The physical manifestation of the Tarot deck that you are holding in your hands is that 'missing' Earth Element. The combinations found in the seventy-eight cards of the Tarot deck represent the sum total of the potential in the universe. When you shuffle the cards, it is like the big bang is happening. When matter falls into the black hole, it comes out in a new universal big bang on the other side.

10 What causes the wheel to spin? Time is the result of motion. Without motion, there is no time. The central point of the

spinning wheel is motionless, therefore timeless. Can you spin the Earth around just by walking on it? Everyone is their own center of the universe. Without perception, does the universe exist at all? Does thought create the universe? Do decisions create parallel universes?

11 What about balance? It makes sense logically to think that all things have their equal and opposite. Time flows forward and backward simultaneously. The intersection of the Past and Future is the eternal "now". The mind can time travel.

12 What about sacrifice and time? Why does it take so long to get what I want? This depends on concentration, motivation, and action. The more you focus your energy on a task, the faster it will happen. An understanding of when to take action and when not to take action is gained by using Tarot Alchemy.

13 What is death? It is the separation of spirit and matter, the separation of energy from matter. Death is the doorway between the worlds of spirit and matter.

14 What will be the result of combining the twenty-two cards of the Major Arcana? There are 231 combinations! This book focuses on the reactions and interactions between and among the twenty-two cards of the Major Arcana. I make no distinction in the order of the two cards that I am looking at. I treat the Fool and the Magician the same as the Magician and the Fool. This can make a bit of a difference in an actual Tarot reading. Intuition is advised so that you know which connection makes the most sense. Usually, both directions of the flow of energy are possible and are worth examining. The sequence in which Tarot cards are drawn can give an indication of the energy flow in time and space. However, for clarity, this should be specified in the question.

15 What obstacles must be overcome? How many cards should be drawn? Should I use a Tarot spread with positional meanings? Should I use the Tarot as an oracle? Is it easy and efficient to

ask for specific pieces of information one at a time? Does a general reading help? Sometimes a framework of where things will happen can give additional information.

16 Destructive energy. What about opposite combinations? For example, The Tower and The Moon would cancel out the effects of each other in a Tarot reading.

17 I use the Tarot cards as an oracle. In future writings, I will give some examples of Tarot spreads, such as the Pyramid Tarot reading, which uses all seventy-eight Tarot cards! Should I use the entire Tarot deck or just the twenty-two cards of the Major Arcana? One way to choose three Major Arcana is to keep selecting Tarot cards from the full deck until you have three Major Arcana. If you can do this in just three cards, it will happen sooner. If it takes thirty or forty cards before you get three, then it may take longer. Or you can separate the deck and only use twenty-two cards. This book analyzes the Major Arcana, so using just twenty-two cards will be fine.

18 Intuition. What about strange Minor Arcana combinations that are unexpressed combinations of the Zodiac? What about Sun + Earth or Venus + Water? Are these combinations expressed in the Major Arcana? Some Tarot cards in the Minor Arcana are reflections (on a lower scale) of Major Arcana cards. For example, the Moon card is Pisces, which is Water and Jupiter. The Four of Cups is also Water and Jupiter, so it is similar. Some combinations in the Minor Arcana are not present in the Major Arcana. For example, the Four of Pentacles is Jupiter and Earth. This is not reflected in the Major Arcana and would usually indicate a mundane or common energy that is available to us here on Earth. The Four of Pentacles can represent property or a house. However, by recognizing that the Four of Pentacles is merely Earth and Jupiter, an analysis can still be made when one is combining it with a Major Arcana or other Minor Arcana card.

19 Revelation. Here are the 231 paragraphs. These are my interpretations. Add your own too based on experience.

20 Karma: Cause and Effect. The Tarot reveals the effect of choice on the universe. Every time a choice is made, a new universe is created. This has been proven by quantum mechanics, string theory, cosmology, and new theories of parallel universes.

21 Conclusion: Manifestation and Completion. I hope you have a better understanding of how to analyze a Tarot reading and gain a better understanding of yourself and your own motivations. If you know how to understand the signs and wonders around you, you can understand the wonders of your own mind and spirit. Magic is the art and science of causing changes to occur in conformity with the will. Are you a magician? What will you do with your own spiritual energy? What is the role of dark energy and dark matter in the universe? Has science proven the existence of spiritual energy? Is this dark energy? Or is it dark matter? If $E = m \star c^2$, is it also true for dark matter? Dark energy $=$ dark matter $\star$ c^2

Thank you for listening to these rambling thoughts. I apologize as this is my first attempt at writing a book. Hopefully in the future my writing style will improve so that the thoughts I am trying to convey will be less confusing.

CONCLUSION

So here is the end result of my efforts. It is the complete binary analysis of the Major Arcana using the principles of Tarot Alchemy to reveal the meaning of the interaction. There are 231 possible combinations of the Tarot cards in the Major Arcana, so I have written 231 paragraphs to reflect this fact. I hope it helps you in your search for truth.

I have written these 231 paragraphs as a starting point. In the future, I plan to do the entire Tarot deck of 3,003 combinations! It will be a big job, and I may need some help from you! The subject of this book is the complete analysis of the twenty-two cards in the Major Arcana, that is, each Tarot card combined with every other. This leads to exactly 231 possible combinations, so I have written 231 paragraphs describing these reactions and interactions. The number $231 = 3 \star 7 \star 11$, a very cool number! Just as a good chef mixes the ingredients to create a gourmet meal, the Tarot cards are mixed to create an image of the future.

The Fool (0) + The Magician (1)

Air + Mercury. This combination is the result of knowledge on thought. It is the use of logic. It is the manipulation of thought. It is communication with the true higher self. It is control over the four elements and the spirit world. Knowledge only exists in the realm of thought. A spiritual child. Reality is only the reflection of the truth. The Fool card represents free will, while the magician card suggests communication and control over the elements. Communication can affect free will. The union of spirit and mind. Spirit and free will are in harmony. The spirit is controlled by the will. The greatest gift we have ever been given is free will. A very young person. The letters I R A J S are indicated. This 0-1 combination represents the binary (on-off) nature of the universe. The potential becoming the kinetic.

The Fool (0) + The High Priestess (2)

Air + Moon. This combination is the influence of intuition and memory on free will. We learn through experience and memory. There are hidden influences that affect our choices. We have instincts. This is a positive combination for spiritual advancement through the subconscious mind. The time period of the new moon is indicated. Our actions and choices will be remembered in our subconscious mind forever. Our memories also influence our choices. This is the dream world. This combination points to karma expressed through dreams. This is a message from your higher self through dreams. The letters I R B K T are indicated.

The Fool (0) + The Empress (3)

This is Air + Venus. This combination is the spirit interacting with the feminine principle. The Empress card points to pregnancy. It is the interaction of the higher self with the mother during pregnancy. It is the spirit of an unborn child. Spirit and love come from the same source. Spirit creates love. Beautiful thoughts and daydreams. Artistic inspiration. This combination is love that has been activated and understood. This can point to musical instruments using wind or air. It is beautiful music played from a flute or wind chimes. It is also be sweet-smelling perfumes or pleasant odors. The odors of cooking food. Can be a female comedian, clown, joker or immature woman. Vibration. The letters I R C L U are indicated.

The Fool (0) + The Emperor (4)

Air + Aries (Mars + Fire) The decision making process. An intense fire. Free will, but also foolishness. A strict authority figure that lacks wisdom. Thoughts that lead to destructive behavior, but perhaps for a good reason. This combination suggests the police or the military. An authority figure that makes unwise decisions. A soldier who follows orders without question. Aggressive thoughts and behaviors. Intellectual competition. Courage. The prodigal son. The fool lacks the discipline of the Emperor. Experience will lead to control of thought. The letters I R D M V are indicated.

The Fool (0) + The Hierophant (5)

Air + Taurus (Venus + Earth). Intellectual books. The effects of organized religion on the spirit. Writing a book. An educational setting. Art, nature and creativity. A carefree relationship. An extravagant wedding. Natural beauty and flowers. A calm sweet natural setting. The smell of flowers. Love is the force that makes dreams come true. The breath of life. A student-teacher relationship. A lazy student. A class-clown. Art school. A mentor. The manifestation of thought through art and love. The educational process. The letters I R E N W are indicated.

The Fool (0) + The Lovers (6)

Air + Gemini (Mercury + Air). Lovers in the act of conception. Innocent, thoughtful love. Soul mate. Ideal marriage. Union of mental opposites. This combination is the union of the male and female sides of brain. Considering all sides of an argument. Intellectual connections between lovers. Conception of a new child. Using light as a method of communication. The vacuum of space. Two strands of DNA, which are the recipe of life. A synergistic relationship. Intelligent relationship. Telepathy. Love at first sight. The union of conflicting ideas that creates something new. This is the creative aspect of making a decision. Every time a decision is made, a new universe is created. How a love relationship affects thought. How a love relationship transforms thought. The letters I R F O X are indicated. These two cards are strongly linked through the element of Air.

The Fool (0) + The Chariot (7)

Air + Cancer (Moon + Water) The mind combined with the spiritual vehicle. The use of the imagination to transform thought. Astral travel. The union of mind and spirit. It is being conscious of the soul. Thoughts that are influenced by spiritual or emotional energies. Activity at night. Do not travel without planning first. Meditation and contemplation of the connection between thought and intuition. Unconscious thoughts and dreams. A journey that brings spiritual progress. Roller coasters and bumper cars. Fun transportation. Spiritual and psychic energy that is in harmony with the mind. A moment of 'accidental' discovery. Making progress accidentally. The letters I R G P Y are indicated. These two cards are weakly linked through numerology. The Fool = 0 = 9 = Moon = Cancer = Chariot.

The Fool (0) + Strength (8)

Air + Leo (Sun + Fire) Positive behaviors linked directly to thought. It is intentional and positive behavior. Growth of thought and increase of knowledge and skill. Creative self-expression. Self-control leads to intellectual enlightenment. Invisible forces. Energy that travels through the air. Radio or television waves. Electromagnetic waves of radiation. Changes in breathing patterns or air quality will improve health. Hot dry air is indicated. This combination points to good health and the ability to fight off disease. Intellectual pursuits will give good health to the mind as well as the body. Exercise the mind as well as the body. Solve mathematical puzzles and use logic more often to improve health. Spiritual light and strong spiritual energy. The role of light in vision and understanding. How light affects thought. A brightly burning spiritual flame. The Holy Spirit. Youth and young people. The letters I R H Q Z are indicated.

The Fool (0) + The Hermit (9)

Air + Virgo (Mercury + Earth). Manifestation of thought. Will. Thought. Creation of true will. Logical order, making decisions based on wisdom. The effect of thought on free will. Knowledge changes your free will and decision making process. Making a choice based on logic. Making wise choices. We have the free form concept that is developed through the laws of nature in the process of creation. Manifestation using the spoken word. Vibration of magical words to bring about manifestation. Communicating your Will. Praying out loud. Commanding something to be. Giving names to people and things, for example when Adam named the animals. Writing a book. An email. A telephone conversation. The sense of hearing. Someone who is conceited. A know it all. The letters I and R are indicated. These two cards are strongly linked through numerology. 0=9.

The Fool (0) + The Wheel of Fortune (10)

Air + Jupiter Constructive thoughts. Important decisions that change your life. Images in the mind. Intelligence. Positive Karma. Free will spins the wheel of karma. Our decisions create our luck and fortune through karma. Not considering the effects and results of your actions. Not caring what happens in your future. Random energy. The soul that is subject to karma. The invisible or hidden nature of destiny. A windy Thursday. Blessings that you receive due to karma. The karma of thought. Even thoughts can change your destiny. The letters I R A J S are indicated.

The Fool (0) + Justice (11)

Air + Libra (Venus + Air). Musical inspiration. The logic behind music. How music affects thought. Religious singing or chanting. Contemplation of art. Thinking about beautiful things. Harmonious balance and the nature of thought. Artistic inspiration. Poetry. Mathematical inspiration, Eureka! Beauty that inspires thought. Color. Loves effects on the thoughts. The goal of life is to balance karma. The universe is created out of the karma of the suns and stars. Disorder seeks balance. Every decision has a consequence. The letters I R B K T are indicated. These two cards are strongly linked through the element of Air.

The Fool (0) + The Hanged Man (12)

Air + Water Creativity. Repulsion. Two invisible elements. These two elements naturally like to separate. It is clouds and bubbles. Energy without structure or function. Unconscious sacrifice. Doing good work as a natural instinct. The linkage between thought and emotion. Emotional perception. A carefree attitude that suddenly ceases. A serious event that suddenly 'wakes you up' out of a silly mood. The ability to mature due to harsh circumstances. The loss of youth. A combination of trust and respect. A deep spiritual learning experience. The delayed reaction between thought and emotional response. The interplay of thought and emotion. The letters I R C L U are indicated.

The Fool (0) + Death (13)

Air + Scorpio (Mars + Water). Freewill and karma. Reflected perception. The separation of the spirit from the body. Elevated consciousness through karma. The spiritual doorway. Death of a thought, forgetfulness, releasing an idea from the mind. Mental detachment. An idea moving from one phase to the next. Spirit set free from the body. Eventually, the life of the fool will end. An out of body experience. Reincarnation. Inspired by spirits or ghosts. Aggressive thoughts motivated by destructive emotions such as suicide. A hex. Poison gas and places that smell of death. Visions or thoughts of murder or death. The letters I R D M V are indicated.

The Fool (0) + Temperance (14)

Air + Sagittarius (Jupiter + Fire). Thought, construction, and passion. Your ideals. Prayer and contact with the angels. Protective energy. Constructive, impassioned thoughts. The scaffolding of your ideas. Receiving karmic blessings for a good decision. Holy inspiration. Thought are the arrows of the mind. This combination can also be a vision or dream. It is speaking in tongues. Baptism by fire, the gift of the Holy Spirit. Faith healing. The solution to a problem obtained through angelic intervention. Prayers that lead to correct decision making. Explorers. Creative thoughts. The abstract mind. Solving a problem in your mind first and then following through with successful action. The letters I R E N W are indicated.

The Fool (0) + The Devil (15)

Air + Capricorn (Saturn + Earth). Obsessive thoughts. Selfish thoughts. Addictions and temptations. Possession. Thought, time, and manifestation. Thoughts that travel through time. Black magic. The time lag between thought and deed. Evil exists only in the heart of men. Selfish decisions or thoughts. Doubtful and fearful thoughts that cause evil actions. Making a decision that leads to darkness. Ignorance that leads to darkness. Giving in to temptation out of ignorance. Not seeing the danger in a choice that is made impulsively. Temptation. The freedom to choose evil over good. The letters I R F O X are indicated.

The Fool (0) + The Tower (16)

Air + Mars. Loss of faith. Proud, conquering thoughts. Malevolent thoughts. Taking a leap of faith. Destructive choices. The Tower of Babble was a competition with God, and is destroyed by lightening. Chain of command in thought processes. Impulsive behavior. Thought control for selfish things. The electrical impulse that our thoughts create. Brain washing. Brain electrochemistry. Language difficulty. Dementia. Language is to thought what colors are to light. The Tower is to language what a prism is to light. Choosing to learn a different language. The effects of anger on thought. The letters I R G P Y are indicated.

The Fool (0) + The Star (17)

Air + Aquarius (Saturn + Air). Thought process as it moves through time. A revelation or divine message. Thought bridging vast distances between stars. Looking into the past. Time travel, predicting dates accurately. The star is a sun from a distant perspective. Thinking from a distant point of view. Seeing a vision of the future. Existing in all time points simultaneously. Thoughts you have today will affect the future and the past. The relationship between thoughts, time and distance. A darky smoky wind. The speed of light. The letters I R H Q Z are indicated. These two cards are strongly linked through the element of Air.

The Fool (0) + The Moon (18)

Air + Pisces (Jupiter + Water). Lucid dreams. Thoughts influenced by lunar cycles, or by the unconscious. Nine is the number of the Moon card, which can correspond with the nine months of pregnancy. This combination represents an idea in gestation or spiritual contemplation. Constructive energy through Archetypal symbols. Mentally exploring levels of psychic consciousness. Abstract thought. Creative visualization. The letters I and R are indicated. These two cards are weakly linked through numerology, as 0 = 9.

The Fool (0) + The Sun (19)

Air + Leo (Sun + Fire) A windy Sunday. Carefree, happy and successful. Fresh air brings healing. Spend time in the light of the Sun. Positive behaviors that are the result of intentional thought. The ability to control thoughts. Sending energy through thoughts. The ability to read and understand the thoughts of another person. The soul living in the garden of Eden. A peaceful happy life. A protected soul that is on the right path. The innocence of youth. Truth and absolute faith. Entertainers, singers and dancers. The court jester. A comedian. The letters I R A J S are indicated.

The Fool (0) + Judgement (20)

Air + Fire A very active combination. Thoughts that lead to direct actions. A bright hot fire with lots of bright light. Awareness of the soul. Old ideas that are brought back to life. The ability to forgive someone. It is the light travelling through the vacuum of space. Thinking carefully about your actions before performing them. The interplay between action and thought. Actions that change thoughts. Patterns of behavior that are learned. Someone with an overactive mind. A hyperactive person. Rebirth and reincarnation that is a direct result of your own decisions. The letters I R B K T are indicated.

The Fool (0) + The World (21)

Air + Saturn The effects of time on thought. Thought energy can time travel. Thoughts exist in all time periods. This combination is the Alpha and the Omega. The first and the last. The Fool has completed his journey and is ready to advance. Notice the big 0 present on the World card. It represents the cycle starting over again. It is infinity. Free will takes place in time. There is a time lag between thought and manifestation. The interplay between time and thought. Accidental success and achievement. Being in the right place at the right time. Lucky timing. The soul trapped in the body and trapped in time. The letters I R C L U are indicated.

The Magician (1) + The High Priestess (2)

Mercury + Moon. Two planetary forces. Communication and logic applied to intuition and psychic knowledge. Interpretation of dreams. Seeing and interpreting visions. The analysis of the subconscious. Astral projection and scrying. Mastery over the elements guided by the holy spirit. Here the magician is accessing hidden knowledge. Creative but secretive. The male and female aspects of reality. The duality of the universe. Mirrors. An innocent couple. The left and right sides of the brain. The interplay between conscious and unconscious thought. The Magician and High priestess will become the Emperor and Empress after they are married. The letters A J S B K T are indicated.

The Magician (1) + The Empress (3)

Mercury + Venus The union of art and science. The left and right side of the brain. The mother and son relationship. Creative and productive. Talented and fruitful. A handsome man. An intelligent woman. A woman pregnant with a son. The scientific side of art. The structure behind poetry and music. A man married to an older woman. Beautiful jewelry. Professing your love for someone. A confident, talented woman. A creative handsome young man. A fertility doctor or successful fertility treatment. The letters A J S C L U are indicated.

The Magician (1) + The Emperor (4)

Mercury + Aries (Mars + Fire) Aggressive words or intimidation. Masculine and fatherly. Creative and productive. A talented advisor. The Magician becomes the Emperor. It is the father-son relationship. Actions are clear and dangerous. The will is carried out through force. A stepfather, godfather or a boss that becomes a good friend. Wednesdays during Aries are indicated. The male aspect of the universe. Natural talent and ability. Treaties between two countries. The Science behind war. Studying martial arts. A military doctor. Military communications. The letters A J S D M V are indicated.

The Magician (1) + The Hierophant (5)

Mercury + Taurus (Venus + Earth) Wednesdays during Taurus. A talented student. A science book. A medical school. An artist. A connection to churches or religious books. The Holy Bible. A young priest or teacher. A scientist with a creative or artistic side. A young person who has new ideas that may conflict with the older establishment. New knowledge that reveals true natural laws. The laws of nature. Gifted blessings. Seating areas in churches. The letters A J S E N W are indicated.

The Magician (1) + The Lovers (6)

Mercury + Gemini (Mercury + Air). Wednesdays during Gemini. Magic words. The power of speech to influence thought. Ideas, thought and will power. Hypnotist. A motivational speaker. The male aspect of the love union. Communication between lovers. The magic wand. The ink pen, the phallus. Manifesting power through vibration and resonance. Healing a mental illness. Marriage counseling. An aphrodisiac or a love potion. Intelligence that is synthetic. Sexual healing. Sexually inspired thought. This combination can also point to bisexuality. The letters A J S F O X are indicated. These two cards are strongly linked through the planet Mercury.

The Magician (1) + The Chariot (7)

Mercury + Cancer (Moon + Water) Wednesdays during Cancer. Traveling in the spirit body. Astral travel. Using magic words to control the astral vehicle. The Chariot follows the will of the driver. Messages from dreams and the unconscious realm. Travel for medical reasons. An ambulance. The creative progress. Communication is important during travel. It is time to write something mathematical or geometric. A symbol is created. Talent will be recognized and there will be advancement. The chariot of the soul has a knowledgeable and talented driver. It is the conscious use of spiritual power. It can represent the abdomen. Railway stations. The letters A J S G P Y are indicated.

The Magician (1) + Strength (8)

Mercury + Leo (Sun + Fire) Wednesdays during Leo. Taking medicine. Doctors and healers of all types. Science and truth. Knowledge that spreads quickly and changes society. A powerful, talented person. Someone who is gifted and talented enough to use his powers and strengths. Putting knowledge to successful use. Practice makes perfect. Someone with strong mathematical talents. Someone with a quick wit and intellect. A skillful doctor or scientist. Emblems and symbols. The letters A J S H Q Z are indicated. These cards are weakly linked through numerology as the Strength card = 8 = Mercury = The Magician.

The Magician (1) + The Hermit (9)

Mercury + Virgo (Mercury + Earth) Wednesdays during Virgo. Manifestation of thought through the spoken word. Thoughts that are made manifest. The wise man and his apprentice. The wise wizard teaching his skills to the younger student. It is the master-student relationship. Solitude leads to creative thinking that is used to solve problems in a unique way. A very intelligent person. Very good with numbers and math. Someone able to solve puzzles and analyze people quickly. Someone with a strong memory and capable of complicated thoughts. A genius or savant. Scientists. Words, alphabets and vocabulary. The letters A J S I R are indicated. These two cards are strongly linked through the planet Mercury.

The Magician (1) + The Wheel of Fortune (10)

Mercury + Jupiter Wednesday night at midnight. Creative thought. The Wheel and the four elements are balanced. When the four elements are balanced, the wheel of fortune spins. Gifted and lucky. A positive future and destiny that is under control. The ability to change destiny. The mind can influence karma. Creating good luck through the use of skill. Speaking aloud what you want. A fortunate and talented person. A creative person. An architect. The interaction of the four elements causes the wheel of destiny to spin. Messages that bring good news. Good news from a doctor or scientist. A bank teller. The letters A J S are indicated. These two cards are strongly linked through numerology. The Magician = 1 = 10 = Wheel of Fortune.

The Magician (1) + Justice (11)

Mercury + Libra (Venus + Air) Wednesdays during Libra. Finding hidden patterns in nature. Mathematics that creates beauty. The logical aspect of music. Songs and singing. Balancing the four elements and using balance for manifestation. A gifted lawyer and good orator. Communication that brings the truth. Someone who makes the right decision quickly. Someone who can think quickly. A musical genius. A poet or songwriter. The sense of hearing. The spoken word. An excellent singer. The voice and vocal chords. The letters A J S B K T are indicated.

The Magician (1) + The Hanged Man (12)

Mercury + Water The emotion of courage. Sacrifice of the will. Giving up individuality to conform to a group. Losing the ego. The union of logic and emotion. It is someone who is able to express their emotions. Communication through emotions, not words. Limited creativity. Unused talent. Someone who is not living up to their full potential. Emotional distractions to a task of the mind. A hypnotist or mentalist. Someone who likes to play emotional games with people and influence them through calculated methods. Intentional emotional manipulation of others. A message that was lost. A delay in receiving important information. The letters A J S C L U are indicated.

The Magician (1) + Death (13)

Mercury + Scorpio (Mars + Water). Wednesdays during Scorpio. Logic, drive, emotion. The Lazarus effect. Ritual magic to contact the spirit world. When the four elements are balanced, spirit is created and revealed. Necromancy. Communication with spirits. Messages received from the spirit world. The death of the ego through ritual magic. Head versus heart. Crossing over into the spirit world. Using the energy of the dead. Using negative death magic. Anger and violent will towards others. The Magician undergoes a spiritual transformation. Someone who dies during surgery. A doctor trying to control death. A mortician. The letters A J S D M V are indicated.

The Magician (1) + Temperance (14)

Mercury + Sagittarius (Jupiter + Fire) Wednesdays during Sagittarius. The magician is communicating with his hold guardian angel. Prayer brings wisdom and knowledge. Communication with the angels. A prayer for protection. Being conscious of spiritual beings. A gift or talent that is controlled through balance. Not being too extreme with your desires. Using your talents for the benefit of others. A hunter. Advertising. Constructive ideas that are acted upon. Adventurers. Expressing good will and favors to others. A very flexible person. Someone who can adjust to a situation quickly. A positive orator. Someone who gives self-help lectures. A motivational speaker or prophet. Someone who has seen the angels. A religious sermon. The letters A J S E N W are indicated.

The Magician (1) + The Devil (15)

Mercury + Capricorn (Saturn + Earth) Wednesdays during Capricorn. Be sure not to use your talents for evil. Do not lie or gossip. There is temptation to use your gifts for selfish reasons. There is a danger of pride. Talents and gifts that are wasted. Someone who is not applying themselves. Laziness. A powerful person with a bad reputation. Manipulating other people through lies. Drugs and narcotics. Disease and illness. Thievery. Mercury is the God of thieves. A master criminal. A self-centered arrogant person. The letters A J S F O X are indicated.

The Magician (1) + The Tower (16)

Mercury + Mars. Tuesday night at midnight. Aggression with knowledge. Ambition. A quick attack based on intelligence. Quick and powerful force to bring about change. Military strategy or intelligence. Military medicine. An impulsive doctor. Using electricity in medical treatments. Electronic devices such as cell phones and televisions. Knowledge received through passion. Gnosis. The ability to call down lightening. The ability to call down and direct powerful energy. Psychic energy that has a purpose. Arguments. Aggressive talk. The use of swear words. A military doctor. Poisons used during war. A powerful dangerous person. A person who can speak multiple languages. Radio and television broadcasts. The letters A J S G P Y are indicated.

The Magician (1) + The Star (17)

Mercury + Aquarius (Saturn + Air) Wednesdays during Aquarius. A creative talented person who has faith in his own abilities. An intelligent person that can see the future. A Tarot card reader. The spoken word. Nervousness and anxiety. Faith will bring success and creativity. A problem will be solved in an unusual way. Something from the distant past will be found. The ability to influence people with the mind. Communicating with someone who is far away. The letters A J S H Q Z are indicated. The Star card is weakly linked to the Magician card because 17 = 8 = Mercury.

The Magician (1) + The Moon (18)

Mercury + Pisces (Moon + Water) Wednesdays during Pisces are indicated. It is knowledge, communication and intuition. It is communication with the spiritual self. It is the use of psychic energy in ritual magic. It is logic applied to intuition. It is the ability to understand your unconscious self. It is the logical understanding of psychic energy. It is a logical acceptance of the spiritual self. Spiritual communication will take place. Listen for a message from a spirit guide. Anxieties. The energy of surface tension on a liquid. Surface tension energy is similar to gravity. The emotional response to a spiritual revelation. Tears of joy. Using your skills to benefit others. Being charitable. The letters A J S I R are indicated.

The Magician (1) + The Sun (19)

Mercury + Sun. A very positive combination. Mercury is the closest planet to the sun. It is also the fastest. It is swift communication and spreading good news. It is healing. Doctors and hospitals will solve the problem. This combination is good for healing and the healing profession. A baby boy is born. A healthy child. Using your talents to help others. Letting your light shine. A happy successful talented person. Activity during the daylight hours will be beneficial. Someone who is quick to heal. A disease that is cured. It is accuracy and discovering the truth. Vision and the role of light in perception. This combination is ambition and ambitious people. The letters A J S are indicated. These two cards are strongly linked through numerology. The Sun = 19 = 10 = 1 = Magician.

The Magician (1) + Judgement (20)

Mercury + Fire. Transformational knowledge. Raising the dead. However, the magician is consciously aware of this turn of events and is directing it. The Magician has power over life and death. Mercury and fire have healing properties that together bring enlightenment. Prometheus is represented here, indicating control over fire. Transformation on two levels, physical and astral. When the 4 elements are balanced, the angels can be invoked. Electrons moving through a circuit board. The heat of laser beams, exothermic energy moving through a logical pathway. A good time to undertake a difficult intellectual task. It is the heat and light that is created by knowledge. Knowledge is exothermic. An important report or essay on a topic. The letters A J S B K T are indicated.

The Magician (1) + The World (21)

Mercury + Saturn The effects of time on thought. A successful talented person. The ability to reach your goals. Gifted and talented. Assured success. Someone who always gets what they want. The ability to manifest your desires. A materialistic person. Someone focused on outward appearance. The ability to know when something will happen. Someone with a good sense of time. A very successful doctor or famous scientist. The study of time and cosmology. The animals. A weather forecaster. The letters A J S C L U are indicated.

The High Priestess (2) + The Empress (3)

The Moon + Venus The mother and daughter relationship. Love and psychic energy combined. A love spell. A fertility spell. The time period of the new moon will be fertile. It is abundance and success found through the use of intuition or instinct. Natural motherly instincts. A secret pregnancy. The natural instinct of motherly love. Abundance as the result of innocence. Female puberty. A daughter will be born. An intuitive person. A natural talent or spiritual gift in the form of art or music. Music or art that leads to spiritual inspiration. The letters B K T C L U are indicated.

The High Priestess (2) + The Emperor (4)

The Moon + Aries (Mars + Fire) An authority figure who acts on instinct or intuition. Aggressive dreams or uncomfortable feelings. The time period of the new moon during Aries is indicated. The father and daughter relationship. A sensitive leader. Military secrets or government cover-ups. Someone with a restless mind. Someone who has difficulty in sleeping. A nervous or aggressive person who may not be aware of his effect on others. The letters B K T D M V are indicated.

The High Priestess (2) + The Hierophant (5)

The Moon + Taurus (Venus + Earth) Mondays during Taurus. Secret knowledge. Books of wisdom and art. Spiritual books and books about churches and nuns. It is purification. Knowledge and education. Learning secrets. Artistic and intuitive creativity. A natural artist. The time period of the new moon during Taurus. A surprise or secret admirer. An anonymous gift. Joining a secret organization. Personal secrets that may be sexual. Female intuition. A girl's school. Artistic inspiration. A nun at a convent. A pristine land. A field that has only recently been plowed. Purification of the body. The letters B K T E N W are indicated.

The High Priestess (2) + The Lovers (6)

Moon + Gemini (Mercury + Air) Mondays during Gemini. Intuition, psychic energy, with thought, communication and healing. The new moon during Gemini. Twin thoughts in your dreams. Communication through dreams. Healing using thought and psychic energy. Hypnosis, psychology— communicating with the unconscious. Using the intuition to solve a scientific or mathematical problem. Woman having psychic experience through union of opposites. The spiritual inspiration for sex in dreams. Having dreams about your soul mate. The letters B K T F O X are indicated.

The High Priestess (2) + The Chariot (7)

The Moon + Cancer (Moon + Water) Mondays during Cancer. Psychic energy. Visions and dreams. Contact with the spirit world. The use of intuition. Spiritual travel. Travel during the time of the new moon. Spiritual progress. Travel that leads to answers. Travelling to an unknown place. Someone who is confident and in control of their situation. Activity at night. Travel at night. Spending time near the water at night. Mirrors and reflection. Fountains. The letters B K T G P Y are indicated. These two cards are strongly linked through the Moon.

The High Priestess (2) + Strength (8)

The Moon + Leo (Sun + Fire) Mondays during Leo. Activities that are balanced between the conscious and unconscious mind. Someone with strong prophetic or healing powers. Mental stress that is relieved. This can be a sexual combination. Vivid dreams that are remembered. A strong female. The time period of the new moon during Leo. The ability to keep secrets and show restraint. Spiritual advancement. Compassion. Mind over matter. The Placebo effect. The letters B K T H Q Z are indicated.

The High Priestess (2) + The Hermit (9)

Moon + Virgo (Mercury + Earth). Holy books. The gift of prophecy. Visions of a spiritual teacher. The Holy Guardian Angel. Virginity and chastity. Using physical media to communicate or commune with messages from the unconscious. Auto writing. Emotionally motivated writing. Vibration that communicates magic words. A dream diary, a novel, or play. The ability to read omens and signs. A wise, intuitive person. A young girl who is close to a teacher or mentor. Trusting your instincts to guide your decision making process. Using a combination of intuition and experience. The letters B K T I R are indicated. These two cards are weakly linked through numerology as the Hermit = 9 = Moon = High Priestess.

The High Priestess (2) + The Wheel of Fortune (10)

The Moon + Jupiter Creative visualization. Constructing images in the mind. The use of subconscious power to create. Positive protective psychic energy. Blessings and protection that comes as the result of positive psychic energy. Reflection and the effects of cause and effect on the spirit world. Spiritual laws of physics are different than material ones. The balance of the four elements creates spirit. Your destiny is secret and opportunities unknown. Natural rhythms such as the seasons or night and day that affect the unconscious mind and psychic energy. The letters B K T A J S are indicated.

The High Priestess (2) + Justice (11)

The Moon + Libra (Venus + Air) Mondays during Libra. The Time period of the New moon during Libra. Decisions from the courts that are kept secret. Behind the scenes agreements. Juries that do not have all of the information. Court secrets. Psychic energy must be balanced before it can be used properly. Music will influence the mind. A female lawyer or judge. An innocent, honest decision maker. The letters B K T are indicated. These two cards are linked strongly through numerology as High Priestess = 2 = 11 = Justice.

The High Priestess (2) + The Hanged Man (12)

The Moon + Water It is reflection. It is the pull of the moons gravity that affects the tides on earth. It is the effect of the moon on the tidal forces. It is waves of energy. Secrets that are kept. Unsolved Mysteries. Puzzles that are yet to be solved. Sacrifice can bring psychic power. Meditation and fasting can bring an increase in psychic or prophetic ability. Do not focus too much on your own sadness. Do not share your burdens with others. This combination can point to a time of boredom. Time will seem to move slowly. The letters B K T C L U are indicated.

The High Priestess (2) + Death (13)

The Moon + Scorpio (Mars + Water) This is destructive psychic energy. It can be a curse or the use of black magic. It is destructive emotional attitudes. It is negative emotional states and can point to addictions that have become compulsions. This is negative destructive spiritual energy that is emitted during emotional trauma. It might be inadvertent. It can also be destructive emotions and tears. Negative emotions may have negative spiritual effects. It is ghosts and graveyards. Ghosts and spirits of the dead. The new moon during Scorpio is indicated. It can be spiritual travel and séances. Visions of ghosts and shadows. Witchcraft. The letters B K T D M V are indicated.

The High Priestess (2) + Temperance (14)

The Moon + Sagittarius (Jupiter + Fire) Prayers. Mondays during Sagittarius. The time period of the new moon during Sagittarius. Innocence and moderation. Devotion. A virgin. A timid secretive person. Visions and communication from the angels. Angelic visions. Spiritual gifts given from the angels. Prayers that are answered. A sleepwalker. Charity work. Doing spiritual work. Constructive spiritual activities. Attending religious events. Allergies are indicated. Steam baths. Taking baths or showers for spiritual reasons. Brain activity during sleep. A connection with the Holy Spirit. The letters B K T E N W are indicated.

The High Priestess (2) + The Devil (15)

The Moon + Capricorn (Saturn + Earth) Mondays during Capricorn. Black magic. The time period of the New Moon during Capricorn. Manifesting objects from another time using spiritual energy. Evil dreams. Demonic possession. Addictions and obsessive compulsive behaviors. Evil mysteries. An evil girl. Secrets that cause evil. Hidden evil deeds. Dreams of hell. It is the spirit trapped in the prison of matter. The ripple effect of an evil deed. This combination can also point to coughing or sneezing. The temptation of Eve. The letters B K T F O X are indicated.

The High Priestess (2) + The Tower (16)

The Moon + Mars Destructive psychic energy. A fire or severe storm that happens near the time period of the new moon. Monday night at midnight. Sudden revelation during a dream. Visions that are seen during a moment of fear. The solution to complicated problems comes suddenly through instinct. Secrets and mysteries that are revealed and cause much pain and hardship. Secret codes that are broken during war that lead to disaster. Secrets that become public and damage reputations. Adrenaline. Nightmares or dangerous dreams of fire and lightening. Scary dreams or night terrors. Premonitions of some calamity that will come. The letters B K T G P Y are indicated.

The High Priestess (2) + The Star (17)

The Moon + Aquarius (Saturn + Air) Mondays during Aquarius are indicated. Trust your instincts. This is psychic power and energy. The ability to see the future. A Tarot card reader. Prophetic visions. Dreams that will come true. The ability to sense things that happen far away in distance and time. Spiritual energy that has the ability to time travel. A mysterious or unknown destiny. Making plans for your own future. A time to re-evaluate or re-prioritize your life. A sensitive person. Can point to depression or psychological problems if ill dignified. The letters B K T H Q Z are indicated.

The High Priestess (2) + The Moon (18)

The Moon + Pisces (Jupiter + Water) Mondays during Pisces. Spiritual Visions. The new moon during Pisces. A rainy Monday or Thursday. Emotional visions and psychic energy. Mysteries and spiritual secrets. The ability to understand visions and see the future. Trusting your instincts. Psychic power and witchcraft. Casting spells and intuitively using your psychic gifts. Occult power and following the lunar cycle. Knowing when to take action based upon the moon phases. Dreams that come true. Cycles of hot and cold that affects the emotions. Convents. Creative visualization and the emotional link that is necessary. The letters B K T I R are indicated. These two cards are weakly linked through numerology. The Moon = 18 = 9 = Moon = High Priestess.

The High Priestess (2) + The Sun (19)

The Moon + The Sun An eclipse. Sunday night at midnight. A very powerful combination. The union of the male and female energies in perfect balance and alignment. Giving birth to a daughter. Becoming conscious of your dreams. The ability to understand visions. Psychic power and the ability to manifest your thoughts quickly. Success, happiness and abundance that is kept secret. A successful, humble person. Meeting your soul mate. A day when the Sun and Moon are in the sky together. A positive spiritual union. The left and right side of the brain working in harmony. Spiritual revelations. Meditation brings good health and prosperity. A very fortunate combination. The letters B K T A J S are indicated.

The High Priestess (2) + Judgement (20)

The Moon + Fire Moonlight. Dreams, hypnosis or other psychological activity. REM sleep. Unconscious behaviors. Breathing and heartbeats. Bodily activity that is unconscious, for example digestion. Mysterious transformations. Lucid dreaming. A good memory. Being able to take action based on memory. Memories and ideas from the past that are given new life. Symbols that lead to behavioral changes. A dividing cell. The letters B K T are indicated. These two cards are linked strongly through numerology as the High Priestess = 2 = 20 = Judgement.

The High Priestess (2) + The World (21)

The Moon + Saturn A new moon that falls on a Saturday. The use of psychic energy to manifest your desires. Forgotten dreams that come true later in life. A physical object that brings back memories. The ability to predict the future and understand the past. Success that comes from a mysterious or unknown source. A sudden flash of inspiration that leads to success and rewards. A prophet. Someone who is good at determining how another person will respond. Someone who is in touch with the spirit world. Innocence leads to abundance. This combination represents cycles of time. The letters B K T C L U are indicated.

The Empress (3) + The Emperor (4)

Venus + Aries (Mars + Fire) Fridays during Aries. The classic male / female combination with the element of Fire present. It is behavior and transformation. It is an activated love relationship. It is fire and passion that leads to conception. The Empress is the mother and the Emperor is the father. A very strong marriage and powerful married couple. The president and the first lady. A balance between male and female energy leads to conception. The role of nature in war. Authority figures that appreciate art, music and beauty. Married grandparents. Renewing your wedding vows. A very active married couple. Love conquers all. Lands that have recently been cleared for farming. A recently plowed field or burned field. A forest fire. The letters C L U D M V are indicated.

The Empress (3) + The Hierophant (5)

Venus + Taurus (Venus + Earth) Fridays during Taurus. An older female schoolteacher. A female church leader. This combination points to abundance through education. It is also motherhood. Art, music and beauty schools are indicated. It can also point to books written for or by women. Books about art and music. Listening to music. This combination is strong in matters of love. Grandmothers and pregnancies are also indicated. The color green and the element Earth are indicated. Very fortunate in matters of love. Flowers, farms and gardens are indicated. Precious stones such as emeralds are also indicated. The letters C L U E N W are indicated. These two cards are strongly linked through planet Venus.

The Empress (3) + The Lovers (6)

Venus + Gemini (Mercury + Air) Fridays during Gemini. Inspiration. A love relationship that leads to pregnancy. True love and soulmates. Creation and a fruitful union. The female perspective of the love relationship. A grandmother who is still married to her true love. A mother-in-law. A protective mother. A mother who gives blessings to the marriage of her daughter. The role of the mother at a wedding. The honeymoon. Telling your mother that you love her. The letters C L U F O X are indicated.

The Empress (3) + The Chariot (7)

Venus + Cancer (Moon + Water) Fridays during Cancer. Traveling to visit your mother or traveling with your mother. A productive trip. Travel that leads to abundance and opportunity. Motivated by love. A productive journey and fruitful change. Spiritual progress as the result of artistic inspiration. A trip or journey that leads to a pregnancy. Conception that takes place in a car. Someone who travels a long distance for love. The birth canal. The womb. Taking a vacation or holiday to a beautiful location. Hormonal and emotional changes that take place during pregnancy. The following letters are indicated : C L U G P Y. These two cards are weakly linked through numerology as the Chariot card = 7 = Venus = The Empress card.

The Empress (3) + Strength (8)

Venus + Leo (Sun + Fire) Fridays during Leo. Creative + Healing. Healing through art or music. Abundance through perseverance. Good health. A strong child that is born. A stable pregnancy. Someone who is strong and beautiful. Someone who is spiritually moral that brings abundance. Someone with a healthy sex drive. A mother who demonstrates self-control in matters of health for the safety of their unborn child. Giving up smoking or drinking due to a pregnancy. A female healer or female doctor or nurse. Parks and zoos. A spiritually positive and wise woman. Crowns made of gold and precious stones. The letters C L U H Q Z are indicated.

The Empress (3) + The Hermit (9)

Venus + Virgo (Mercury + Earth) Fridays during Virgo. A lonely woman or single mother. A wise old woman. Knowledge that brings success and abundance. The structure behind art. The union of art and science that is necessary for manifestation. Productive thinking and motherly guidance. A very careful person. Someone who thinks before acting. Isolation that brings artistic or creative inspiration. An intelligent grandmother. Spending time alone in nature. Wheat fields. Writing a love poem or song. The letters C L U I R are indicated.

The Empress (3) + The Wheel of Fortune (10)

Venus + Jupiter Thursday night at midnight. Love is a creative force, not destructive. Where you see people being protected and cared for, you see true love. Beauty brings protection. There is good luck and fertility. It is a time of abundance. The cycle of life and productive opportunities. Nature brings protection and peace. A matriarchal society. She is a wealthy Queen and a wise ruler. A mother figure that is very protective. A mother who passes her wealth and talent to a daughter. A very lucky woman. Casinos or games of chance. The letters C L U A J S are indicated.

The Empress (3) + Justice (11)

Venus + Libra (Venus + Air) Fridays during Libra. Art, music and beauty. The beauty of symmetry and balance. A wise female judge or lawyer. The beauty of intelligence. A lovely singing voice. Love that leads to a stable partnership. A balanced and fruitful person. A strong, intelligent, beautiful woman. A female leader. A female decision maker. Stringed musical instruments. Sweet smells and pleasant odors. The legal aspect of a love relationship. The letters C L U B K T are indicated. These two cards are strongly linked through the planet Venus.

The Empress (3) + The Hanged Man (12)

Venus + Water. Pure love. Someone who feels content. Falling in love with a woman. The emotional response to love. It is the sacrifices that mothers make for their children. Love and emotion are intertwined. This combination represents the conception or formation of emotions. A mother who sacrifices her life for her child. Emotions that lead to fertility and fertility that leads to emotional change. Insemination. Can point to the menstrual cycle. The letters C L U are indicated. These two cards are strongly linked through numerology. The Empress = 3 = 12 = Hanged Man.

The Empress (3) + Death (13)

Venus + Scorpio (Mars + Water). Fridays during Scorpio. This combination is the death of a grandmother, or of an unborn baby. Cycles of nature, especially the Winter. It is the damaging effect of water on nature, for example floods. The destructive aspect of beauty. Female orgasm. Erosion of water on nature to create beautiful formations, like the Grand Canyon. The fertile land after the deluge of a river. An ocean, a waterfall. P.M.S. and menopause. Things that are born in the water. The life-giving gifts of the spring thaw. A miscarriage. This combination represents the womb. The menstrual cycle and blood. The doorway between life and death. This combination can also be an abortion. The letters C L U D M V are indicated.

The Empress (3) + Temperance (14)

Venus + Sagittarius (Jupiter + Fire) Fridays during Sagittarius. Abundance, protection and blessings. Constructive behaviors. Dancing and expressing love. Expressing love in moderation. The abundance of the land and wild game. Food. A balanced approach leads to productivity and abundance. A woman concerned with her appearance and public image. A woman who holds back emotionally, especially from her children. Prayers for fertility. Blessings that come as a result of prayer and the influence of Angels. Your fairy god mother. Can be fashion or fashion designers. The letters C L U E N W are indicated.

The Empress (3) + The Devil (15)

Venus + Capricorn (Saturn + Earth). Fridays during Capricorn. A beautiful clock. A woman who is still beautiful in old age. Temptation by a beautiful woman. Adultery. Married to a beautiful woman. The curse of Eve's fall. Sculptures. Natural beauty that has occurred over time, for example, the formation of the Grand Canyon. A diamond wedding ring. An evil woman. The bride of Satan. An illegitimate child. Sexual perversion and venereal diseases. Ovarian cancer or tumors. Caves and underground passages. A witch. An evil, selfish old woman. The letters C L U F O X are indicated. These two cards are weakly linked through Numerology. The Empress = 3 = Saturn = Capricorn = The Devil.

The Empress (3) + The Tower (16)

Venus + Mars The classic male-female union. Sex. Aphrodisiacs. An unexpected pregnancy. A thunderstorm. The unpredictable nature of the weather. A pregnancy that is suddenly lost. A miscarriage. An impulsive older woman. Love at first sight. A dangerous woman with a lot of power. A matriarchal society. A strong female military leader. A conquering female. A female fighter or boxer. An aggressive woman with a temper. The letters C L U G P Y are indicated. These two cards are weakly linked through numerology. The Tower = 16 = 7 = Venus = The Empress.

The Empress (3) + The Star (17)

Venus + Aquarius (Saturn + Air) Fridays during Aquarius. The effect of time on relationships and how it affects thought patterns. Old and faraway places. Older generations and a family with a long history. Can be infertility or difficulty in pregnancy. A fruitful destiny. Favorable but delayed fertility. Pregnancy in older age. Aging well, beautiful older woman. Can be fashion or fashion designers. Extended beauty. Music or art that inspires faith. Eternal beauty. Delays in giving birth. A child who is not ready to be born. The letters C L U H Q Z are indicated. These two cards are weakly linked through numerology. The Empress = 3 = Saturn = Aquarius = The Star.

THE EMPRESS. THE MOON.

The Empress (3) + The Moon (18)

Venus + Pisces (Jupiter + Water) Fridays during Pisces. Reproduction. Pregnancy. The Empress is a pregnant woman. The Moon card points to the monthly female cycle. A protective form of love. Love is a constructive emotion. Protection and love are indicated. A baby's nursery. A baby born at night. Changes to the physical body during puberty or pregnancy. Changes in consciousness due to pregnancy. Dreams of abundance and fertility. The time period of the Full moon on a Friday. An emotional response to pregnancy. Mothers and grandmothers dreaming of each other. Creative inspiration. Music and art that spring from the unconscious mind. Beauty at night. The letters C L U I R are indicated.

THE EMPRESS. THE SUN.

The Empress (3) + The Sun (19)

Venus + The Sun. This combination represents love and opportunity. It points to interactions that are increasing. You will be meeting more people or interacting with people more frequently or more intensely. Art and creativity will bring healing. There are bright colors. It is vitality and interacting with many people. It can also represent the birth of a healthy, intelligent child. It is a healthy, pregnant woman. It is gold and wealth, both physical and spiritual. It is the wealth of the earth. Gold, minerals and oil. The healing power of love. Taking action under the light of the Sun. Enjoying the beauty of nature during the rising Sun. A vital, healthy, successful older woman. The life principal. The letters C L U A J S are indicated.

The Empress (3) + Judgement (20)

Venus + Fire This combination is the expression of love. Demonstrating your true love for someone. The spring time. The rebirth of the plants and flowers in the spring. A very hot Friday. Actions that show love. Artistic activities such as dancing or playing music. Art and beauty. A forgiving mother. Productive change. Ideas from the past will be renewed. Anything feminine. Sexual pleasure. A warm body. Sexual stimulation. The importance of heat and light in the growth process. Love is baptized by fire. Birth is proof of forgiveness. The letters C L U B K T are indicated.

The Empress (3) + The World (21)

Venus + Saturn Friday night at midnight. Pregnancy at an old age. A successful pregnancy after a time of struggle. Mother Earth and the abundance of the Earth. Precious gems and minerals from the Earth. Art that stands the test of time. Music or some other art form that takes a long time to create. Productivity, abundance and success. A successful, independent mother or grandmother. Creation and fruitful rewards. The longevity of nature. Natural evolution. Food and gardens. Gifts given to man by nature. A bountiful harvest. Farming. Nice weather and the beauty of nature and time. The letters C L U are indicated. These two cards are weakly linked through numerology. The Empress = 3 = 21 = The World.

The Emperor (4) + The Hierophant (5)

Aries (Mars + Fire) + Taurus (Venus + Earth). Tuesdays during Taurus and Fridays during Aries. The union of opposites. Constriction. Following the rules of schools and religion. A school principle or church deacon. A military school or Police academy. Fraternal order of police. Social acceptance. Knowledge being passed on. Military intelligence. Groups of people with a religious component. The Taliban. Government imposed religion. The separation of church and state. The crusades. The Jesuits. Karate or other form of martial arts. A military band. Using nature as a military weapon. The Cusp of Aries / Taurus (April 21st) is indicated. Sheep and shepherds. The letters D M V E N W are indicated. These two cards are weakly linked through numerology. The Hierophant = 5 = Mars = Aries = The Emperor.

The Emperor (4) + The Lovers (6)

Aries (Mars + Fire) + Gemini (Mercury + Air) Tuesdays during Gemini and Wednesdays during Aries. Arguments and aggressive thoughts. The male aspect of the love relationship. A strong, intelligent man. A stable union and a protective partner. The father-in-law. A thoughtful leader who is good at pairing people up. Leadership in the marriage. A marriage ruled by a domineering man. Telling your father that you love him. Taking the initiative in pursuing a love relationship. An aggressive sex act or a rape. The letters D M V F O X are indicated.

The Emperor (4) + The Chariot (7)

Aries (Mars + Fire) + Cancer (Moon + Water) Mondays during Aries and Tuesdays during Cancer are indicated as special days. The effects of aggressive behavior on the unconscious mind. This combination represents the chariots of war. Government vehicles or military tanks. It is the conquering General moving his army forward. It is an aggressive invasion and military progress. Be careful, you may be stopped by the police for speeding! The ability to motivate others. It is spiritual leadership. It is the captain of a ship or plane. The authority of travel. Travel paid for by the government. Leadership brings forward progress. Travel will improve leadership. This can also be a 'control freak'. A car repair shop or auto mechanic. A police car. The letters D M V G P Y are indicated.

The Emperor (4) + Strength (8)

Aries (Mars + Fire) + Leo (Sun + Fire) Tuesdays during Leo and Sundays during Aries. A strong leader with self-control. Fatherhood. A powerful, resourceful leader. Military force. The police force. Demonstrating restraint during war. Following the rules of war. Strong leadership abilities. A brave, confident leader. A father with strong morals. A mighty warrior. A selfless leader who is trying to do the right thing for his followers. Physical activity. Lifting weights and working out. The element of Sulfur. A Kings throne. The letters D M V H Q Z are indicated. These two cards are linked strongly through the element of Fire.

The Emperor (4) + The Hermit (9)

Aries (Mars + Fire) + Virgo (Mercury + Earth) Tuesdays during Virgo and Wednesdays during Aries. A wise, old King or politician. A good leader or military planner but may have poor social skills. A strong person who is difficult to access. Guidance from a father-figure. King Solomon. A leader who has been in power for a long time and has gained wisdom. Spending time planning a strategy of attack. The use of the mind and knowledge in war. Code breakers. A strong, powerful old man. An unmarried career politician or world leader. An intelligent, military strategist. A police chief or general. Manufacturers. Putting experience and good management together to create success. Dry places. The letters D M V I R are indicated.

The Emperor (4) + The Wheel of Fortune (10)

Aries (Mars + Fire) + Jupiter Thursdays during Aries. A leader who comes to power as the result of destiny or karma. Stable opportunities and a strong, conquering destiny. The royal family. A protective, military or political leader. Good advice from a father-figure. The overthrow of a dictator. A strong experienced politician or leader. Abundance and the riches of a King. The karma of war. A truce. A fortress. The letters D M V A J S are indicated. These two cards are weakly linked through numerology as the Emperor = 4 = Jupiter = Wheel of Fortune.

The Emperor (4) + Justice (11)

Aries (Mars + Fire) + Libra (Venus + Air) Fridays during Aries and Tuesdays during Libra. A just leader. The interaction of the police and lawyers. The role of the police and government in the justice system. A strong, but fair leader. Military planning. The air-force. Military aircraft. The supreme court. Can point to the role of women in the military. Feelings of dizziness or vertigo. The use of poison gas as a military weapon. The use of loud noises to cause harm. Barking out orders to your soldiers. The chain of command. Military aggression as the result of a court decision. Breaking the law has consequences. The letters D M V B K T are indicated.

The Emperor (4) + The Hanged Man (12)

Aries (Mars + Fire) + Water A rainy Tuesday. The emotions of anger and disgust. An authority figure with no real power. Sacrifices of the soldier for the benefit of society. Sacrifice during times of war or conflict. A suicide bomber. A man with no children. Someone who is being hard on themselves. Giving up your own happiness for the benefit of those you lead. Keeping your strength hidden. Someone with a strong inner strength. Blood that is spilled. The letters D M V C L U are indicated.

THE EMPEROR.   DEATH.

The Emperor (4) + Death (13)

Aries (Mars + Fire) + Scorpio (Mars + Water). Tuesdays during Aries and Scorpio. Water and Fire are enemies. This combination is the killing ability of the government. The death of a stern parent or strong leader. A political revolution. Tremendous spiritual energy. The assassination of a political leader. The death of a father figure. Tyrants. The casualties of war. Killing your enemy. A leader who destroys any obstacle in his way. A leader who uses death to control others. A fallen soldier. The letters D M V are indicated. These two cards are linked strongly through the planet Mars and strongly through numerology since the Emperor = 4 = 13 = Death.

THE EMPEROR.   TEMPERANCE.

The Emperor (4) + Temperance (14)

Aries (Mars + Fire) + Sagittarius (Jupiter + Fire) Thursdays during Aries and Tuesdays during Sagittarius. An army barracks. This combination represents weapons such as bow and arrow. The colors red and blue are indicated. This is a card of leadership in the spiritual world. It is also spiritual authority. Prayer will lead to Discipline. Archery. Religious discipline. You will receive blessings through discipline. Use control and authority when directing spiritual energy. This combination points to the government, firemen and police. The power of prayer will influence leaders. The protective function of the military or government. It is the priesthood. Bright colors and the spectrum. The letters D M V E N W are indicated. These two cards are linked strongly through the element of Fire and weakly through numerology since the Emperor = 4 = Jupiter = Sagittarius = Temperance = 14 = 5 = Mars = Aries = The Emperor.

The Emperor (4) + The Devil (15)

Aries (Mars + Fire) + Capricorn (Saturn + Earth) Tuesdays during Capricorn, and Saturdays during Aries. A selfish evil ruler. The anti-Christ. A violent warlord. Torture and the dark side of war. Selfishness and greed. An evil ruler. Anger, rape and genocide. A power-hungry politician. A crooked cop or person in power tempted by greed. Pain inflicted by a sadistic person. It can be self-mutilation. A mean, selfish, evil person. A powerful, evil person. The prince of darkness. A powerful property owner. Violent diseases. Diseases of the skin such as boils or pimples that show up on the face. Fever blisters or scars. The letters D M V F O X are indicated.

The Emperor (4) + The Tower (16)

Aries (Mars + Fire) + Mars Tuesdays during Aries. This combination is war. Anything connected to the military. It is an aggressive dangerous person. This combination is Mars + Fire and points to destructive behaviors that might get you into trouble with the authorities! The Tower is fire and electricity. It can point to accidents. It is anger and impulsive behavior and clashes with authority figures. Behaviors may be unpredictable. There is a need for discipline. There is a need to control and regulate destructive behavior. Epilepsy or violent diseases. A dangerous combination. The letters D M V G P Y are indicated. These two cards are linked strongly through the planet Mars.

The Emperor (4) + The Star (17)

Aries (Mars + Fire) + Aquarius (Saturn + Air) Tuesdays during Aquarius and Saturdays during Aries. Someone with a clear vision of the future. Someone who fights for what they want. Planning for the future. A good leader who can predict the future and prepare for it. A destiny that is protected. Stable hopes and prospects. The ability to anticipate the actions of an enemy. Congressmen and Senators. The aftermath of war. Barren places. Destroyed buildings and ruins. Destroyed civilizations. Manufacturers. Blueprints or plans for something that will be created. Developing a tactical strategy to conquer obstacles. A well thought out plan of attack. The letters D M V H Q Z are indicated.

The Emperor (4) + The Moon (18)

Aries (Mars + Fire) + Pisces (Jupiter + Water) Tuesdays during Pisces and Thursdays during Aries. The cusp of Pisces / Aries is indicated (March 21st). The Spring Equinox. Aggressive dreams of war or government leaders. This can also be sleeplessness. A person who is not aware of their competitive nature. Be cautious of a deceptive authority figure. Emotional struggles. A protective authority figure. War and fighting at night. Cycles of aggressive behavior. A neat freak or obsessive compulsive person. Competitions held at night. Adrenaline. A competitive swimmer. Dreams about your father. An intuitive leader takes action by instinct. Aggressive male instincts. A private detective or spy. The letters D M V I R are indicated. These two cards are linked weakly through numerology since the Emperor = 4 = Jupiter = Pisces = The Moon.

129

The Emperor (4) + The Sun (19)

Aries (Mars + Fire) + The Sun Sundays during Aries. Using heat, fire or lasers as a weapon of war. Aggressive activity during the day. Fighting for the right reasons. Good health and vitality. A successful, healthy father. A well respected politician who does his best to help his followers. A spiritual leader. A powerful, important person. A man who is happy when he is leading others and making decisions. A good lawmaker. Someone who stands up for their beliefs. The study of thermodynamics. A vital, healthy, successful older man. Military officers and authority figures. A famous person like Julius Caesar. The letters D M V A J S are indicated.

The Emperor (4) + Judgement (20)

Aries (Mars + Fire) + Fire. Rebirth, renewal, forgiveness. The use of fire in a military way like an explosion. Military decision. A decision to use authority. A manager making a decision. A policeman making a choice. The punishment aspect of the legal process. Use of force to bring manifest judgement. The result of the judgement is pain. A charismatic leader who uses military strength in a justified way, to free the enslaved. The Emperor represents the government, so it is a government decision. A wise leader called upon to make an important decision. Heat or heat exhaustion. Energy. The letters D M V B K T are indicated. These two cards are linked strongly through the element of Fire.

The Emperor (4) + The World (21)

Aries (Mars + Fire) + Saturn Saturdays during Aries. The destructive aspect of time. A leader with good timing. Success as the result of being in the right place at the right time. Success after a struggle. Reaping the rewards of war. A conquering successful leader. To arrest someone. A winner. Rewards from an authority figure. A successful advisor. Good advice that leads to success. A world leader or organization such as the United Nations or NATO. A well-organized structure. A well-timed activity that leads to success. The importance of timing in military activities. The ability to plan for future success. Diamonds and diamond cutters. The letters D M V C L U are indicated.

The Hierophant (5) + The Lovers (6)

Taurus (Venus + Earth) + Gemini (Mercury + Air) Fridays during Gemini and Wednesdays during Taurus. A marriage of true soul mates. The Science behind love. Love is logical and implies union. There is a connection between a school or church and a love relationship. You may meet your true love at a school or church. This is a public, formal unification. The exchange of wedding vows and sex. The consummation of marriage. Music inspires sexual passion. It is erotic music and artwork. It is also a romantic novel or book of erotic imagery. This combination points to beautiful flowers. The cusp of Taurus / Gemini (May 21st) is indicated. Schools and schoolwork. Love songs and poems. The letters E N W F O X are indicated.

The Hierophant (5) + The Chariot (7)

Taurus (Earth + Venus) + Cancer (Moon + Water). Fridays during Cancer and Mondays during Taurus. Artistic motivations from the unconscious. A church or school bus. The study of art therapy. Traveling far away to learn religion or spirituality. A mirror or the beauty of symmetry. Female conception. A school that is far from home. The sounds of rushing water. A waterfall. The beauty of oceans, lakes and rivers. Erosion of the earth by water and erosion of the body by the emotions. The Hierophant is the road that the Chariot travels on. Intuition is connected to education. An auto mechanic school. Learning how to build cars or other vehicles. The letters E N W G P Y are indicated. These two cards are weakly linked through numerology. The Chariot = 7 = Venus = Taurus = Hierophant.

The Hierophant (5) + Strength (8)

Taurus (Venus + Earth) + Leo (Sun + Fire) Fridays during Leo and Sundays during Taurus. A strong student. Medical school. A hard working disciplined student or teacher. Healing through religion. Books that lead to positive self-transformation. The force and power of nature. A sunny day spent outside. The relationship between the sun and nature. Energy that is transformed by nature. A healthy plant or tree and the photosynthesis process. Strong marriages and powerful blessings. A successful proud person. Someone who is respected for their accomplishments. Formal high society. Doing the right thing. Someone with great strength who is able to accomplish their goals. Activities that benefit society. The use of momentum. Sunflowers. School buildings. The letters E N W H Q Z are indicated.

The Hierophant (5) + The Hermit (9)

Taurus (Venus + Earth) + Virgo (Mercury + Earth). Fridays during Virgo and Wednesdays during Taurus. Artistic writings, poetry, songs; things that are written but creative. The union of art and science. The study of art. Geometric art work. Logic applied to art, love, music. Could involve schools, or a church. A professor, a priest, a monk, a mystic. It is a seminary. A wise old teacher. Old books. Old buildings and institutions of learning. Old churches. Secret brotherhoods. Secret societies. Fraternities of learning. Wise church leaders. Books of wisdom. Training the physical body. A skill or talent that takes years of training and practice. Yoga and meditation. Education through ritual and logic. The spoken word. Spiritual songs. A prayer for wisdom. A very conservative person. The letters E N W I R are indicated. These two cards are strongly linked through the element of Earth.

The Hierophant (5) + The Wheel of Fortune (10)

Taurus (Venus + Earth) + Jupiter Thursdays during Taurus. A successful student. Donations to a school or church. Unions that lead to positive opportunity. Education that leads to success. Building a church or school. The marriage of soulmates. Destiny that is changed through education or religion. A creative builder or architect. Creating your own fortune through education and social convention. The appreciation of nature. Understanding your role in society. Safes and bank vaults. The letters E N W A J S are indicated.

The Hierophant (5) + Justice (11)

Taurus (Venus + Earth) + Libra (Venus + Air) Fridays during Taurus and Libra. Law school. A book about art. Music or art school. A creative person. Love poems or romantic novels. A marriage license. A balanced relationship. Female energy. Legal approval. Incense and pleasant odors. Sweet smells and perfumes. Beautiful music or artwork. A stable lawmaker. Wind erosion. A windy day. A stable person with a balanced mind. A beautiful mind and body. Thoughts are made manifest through love. Things made of copper. The letters E N W B K T are indicated. These two cards are linked strongly through the planet Venus.

The Hierophant (5) + The Hanged Man (12)

Taurus (Venus + Earth) + Water. Very emotional. Someone who is polite. Sacrifice for education. A saintly person. Emotional response to physical beauty. The appreciation of nature. Creating emotionally inspired art. Making a donation to charity. Tithing. Sacrificing time or money for church or school. May indicate the time of ovulation. Watering crops. Teacher making sacrifices or teaching by example. A farmer or gardener. Sending flowers to your loved one. A river with lots of fish and wild life. A Waterfall. The river of life. The river sacrifices itself to nourish the land. Stubbornness. The letters E N W C L U are indicated.

The Hierophant (5) + Death (13)

Taurus (Venus + Earth) + Scorpio (Mars + Water) Fridays during Scorpio and Tuesdays during Taurus. A funeral. Attending a wake at a church. The death of a student or teacher. Transformation as the result of education. A divorce. The loss of blessings. A curse. The emotional response to the physical body during sex. Books about the spirit world. Books that lead to spiritual transformation. People who learn from near-death experiences. Finding religion after the death of a loved one. Can be growing poisonous food. Can also point to fertilizer. Dropping out of school or being excommunicated from a church. The letters E N W D M V are indicated. These two cards are weakly linked through numerology as the Hierophant = 5 = Mars = Scorpio = Death.

The Hierophant (5) + Temperance (14)

Taurus (Venus + Earth) + Sagittarius (Jupiter + Fire) Fridays during Sagittarius and Thursdays during Taurus. Conformity through education. Dancing and expressions of beauty. Restraint in relationships. A balanced marriage. A beautiful campfire. Game animals. A religious experience. Musical performances. Books or schools about religion. Prayers and religious leaders. The appearance of angels. Communion and other religious rituals. Altars. Religious schools and education in spiritual matters. Religious charities and social activities connected to churches or schools. Universities. The letters E N W are indicated. These two cards are linked strongly through numerology as The Hierophant = 5 = 14 = Temperance.

The Hierophant (5) + The Devil (15)

Taurus (Venus + Earth) + Capricorn (Saturn + Earth). Fridays during Capricorn and Saturdays during Taurus. Old music, old artwork. Timeless beauty. Classical music. Violence or jealousy in a marriage. Laziness in school. The anti-Christ, the satanic church or evil religion. The worship of idols. Teaching of false doctrines. En evil book. The temptation of spiritual leaders. A false prophet. Old churches. A criminal profiler. The letters E N W F O X are indicated. These two cards are linked strongly through the element of Earth.

The Hierophant (5) + The Tower (16)

Taurus (Venus + Earth) + Mars. Tuesdays during Taurus. Abusing the physical body. For example, anorexia and bulimia. Body building. Martial arts. A bullfight. Books about fighting. West point Military Academy. A cult or dangerous social group. A book about war. A violent overthrow of the status quo. Protests against society. Fighting against convention. Violence that erupts at a school. A forest fire. The letters E N W G P Y are indicated. These 2 cards are weakly linked through numerology. The Hierophant = 5 = Mars = The Tower = 16 = Venus = Taurus = Hierophant.

The Hierophant (5) + The Star (17)

Taurus (Venus + Earth) + Aquarius (Saturn + Air) Fridays during Aquarius and Saturdays during Taurus. Education brings hope and opportunity. Long term study is needed. It is time to write a book or keep a journal. There is a connection to a church or school. Love aids in the manifestation of thought. Favorable blessings and the celebration of hope. A defined life plan. Someone with a clear vision of the future. An intelligent well-educated person. A writer or librarian. A long term view of life and education. The use of color and music to influence time. Colors that fade over time. Artwork that becomes weathered or damaged due to time. Someone with a specific purpose. A person who has problems with public speaking. The letters E N W H Q Z are indicated.

The Hierophant (5) + The Moon (18)

Taurus (Venus + Earth) + Pisces (Jupiter + Water) Fridays during Pisces and Thursdays during Taurus. Night school. Cycles of educational behavior. Reading books at night. A student or teacher with a good memory. A cautious marriage. Beautiful objects that stir the emotions. Books that affect the emotions. Sculptures or fountains. Risky relationships and obscure blessings. A very passive, but creative person. Someone who doubts their own talents. Modesty. Someone who is psychologically stable. Charity organizations. Attending church at night. Social interaction at night. A waterfall or beautiful glacier. A convent. Plants that grow in the water. Things made of coral. The letters E N W I R are indicated.

The Hierophant (5) + The Sun (19)

Taurus (Venus + Earth) + The Sun Sundays during Taurus. Creativity. Art and music that brings healing and inspiration. Spiritual power. Churches and religion. Growth of love, shown in physical form. A gift given in love, probably made of gold. The Wedding ring. Blessings and abundance. Productive relationships. Connections to books, teachers and schools. Healing power taken from nature. It is the sun that gives the plants energy to grow. Photosynthesis. Biology and viruses that travel through nature and in plants. Medicines that can be extracted from plants. Books can lead to enlightenment. Social interaction during the day. The birth of the savior. Bakeries and bakers. The Tree of Life. Knowledge creates life. The letters E N W A J S are indicated.

The Hierophant (5) + Judgement (20)

Taurus (Venus + Earth) + Fire A forest fire. The beautiful aspect of a fire. A candle. Education that leads to forgiveness. Going back to school after a long absence. Repentance and forgiveness from a church. Confession that leads to forgiveness. Beautiful dancing. Art or music that transforms or motivates. Blessings that transform the soul. Renewed relationships. A stubborn, strong-willed person. A teacher who is grading their students. Receiving the holy spirit in a church. The ability to learn about oneself. The letters E N W B K T are indicated.

The Hierophant (5) + The World (21)

Taurus (Venus + Earth) + Saturn. Saturdays during Taurus. Achievement, like graduation or initiation. Time, something that takes a long time to complete. Something you achieve after struggle, like a PhD, or going through an initiation or interview process. Education, learning over a long time period. Honor and recognition of hard work over a long period of time. A stable combination. Marriage after a long engagement. Highly cultured and highly regarded. Secret societies. A successful education. A prestigious international school. Money and material possessions. The study of geology and agriculture. The letters E N W C L U are indicated.

The Lovers (6) + The Chariot (7)

Gemini (Mercury + Air) + Cancer (Moon + Water) Wednesdays during Cancer and Mondays during Gemini. Astral travel. Being conscious of your dreams. Travel a long distance to meet a lover. A loving couple relocates. The Moon is the chariot of love. This is conscious spiritual travel. The love relationships that gives progress to the soul. Instincts. Travel and dreams will lead you to true love. Explorations in a new love relationship. Taking love to the next level. Spiritual awareness and revelation during lovemaking. Making out in a car! The cusp of Gemini / Cancer (June 21st) is indicated. The Summer solstice. A mailman or love letter. The letters F O X G P Y are indicated.

The Lovers (6) + Strength (8)

Gemini (Mercury + Air) + Leo (Sun + Fire) Sundays during Gemini and Wednesdays during Leo. A strong love relationship. Saving oneself for marriage. Communicating and expressing love. Sharing your love with others. A strong relationship and powerful union. Love relationships will heal. Health matters are connected to relationship status. Specific actions based on conscious thought. Intentional actions that strengthen the love relationship. Doing extra work to keep a marriage together. A hot, dry wind. Courtships. The letters F O X H Q Z are indicated. These two cards are linked weakly through numerology. The Lovers = 6 = Sun = Leo = Strength = 8 = Mercury = Gemini = Lovers.

The Lovers (6) + The Hermit (9)

Gemini (Mercury + Air) + Virgo (Mercury + Earth) Wednesdays during Gemini and Virgo. Knowledge + Wisdom. The color orange. Communication. A secret romance. Seeking a love relationship. Showing rather than speaking. The demonstration of love. An older gentleman involved in a love affair. Love letters or love stories. A lonely person who finds love. A secret admirer. A man who falls in love at an old age. Love that stands the test of time. A married couple that respects the vows of chastity until marriage. An old flame may enter your life, but now you may feel like strangers. The letters F O X I R are indicated. These two cards are strongly linked through the planet Mercury.

The Lovers (6) + The Wheel of Fortune (10)

Gemini (Mercury + Air) + Jupiter. Thursdays during Gemini. Constructive thoughts. Blueprints. The framework of thought, the plans. Thoughts that bring prosperity. The karma of thoughts. Love turns the wheel of fate. How love relationships affects karma. This may signify the realization of an idea. Being protective of one's soul mate. Architectural design. Converting thoughts into talismans, or symbols. Constructive criticism. Teaching. Protecting your reputation, asking for help. All relationships are a gamble. Legal contracts. The letters F O X A J S are indicated.

The Lovers (6) + Justice (11)

Gemini (Mercury + Air) + Libra (Venus + Air) Fridays during Gemini and Wednesdays during Libra. A marriage. Balanced love. Planning a wedding. Careful thought about the future of your love relationship. The legal aspect of marriage. A beautiful wedding and love relationship. Successful partnerships. A balanced legal result based on science and mathematics. Something that is mathematically balanced or symmetrical. Court reporters. The letters F O X B K T are indicated. These two cards are linked strongly through the element of Air.

The Lovers (6) + The Hanged Man (12)

Gemini (Mercury + Air) + Water The emotion of love. This combination is someone who is willing to sacrifice himself for a lover. Walking away from a marriage or love relationship. Taking a break in a love relationship. Letting go of someone you love. Stagnant love relationships. Making sacrifices for a loved one. Giving up power and privilege for love. A partnership will be limited or discontinued. A lover who may be a bit too passive. A rainy Wednesday. The ability to communicate with a lover through the use of emotions, not words. The letters F O X C L U are indicated.

The Lovers (6) + Death (13)

Gemini (Mercury + Air) + Scorpio (Mars + Water) Tuesdays during Gemini and Wednesdays during Scorpio. The death of a love relationship. A divorce. The death of a loved one. Loss of love. A partnership that comes to a final end. A person who is still in love with someone who has passed away. A widow or widower. A venereal disease. The letters F O X D M V are indicated.

The Lovers (6) + Temperance (14)

Gemini (Mercury + Air) + Sagittarius (Jupiter + Fire). Wednesdays during Sagittarius and Thursdays during Gemini. It is the use of knowledge and science to create a new technology. It is the understanding of science and mathematics. It is the ability to act on your knowledge. It is a skill that you possess. Communication with a lover over a long distance. It is the use of technology and how it affects your behaviors. It is turning your thoughts into a creation. It is the manifestation of your thoughts. It is taking direct actions to build your dreams. Think before you take action. Plan out your creative process. An ideal soul mate. Using prayer to find your true love. The letters F O X E N W are indicated.

The Lovers (6) + The Devil (15)

Gemini (Mercury + Air) + Capricorn (Saturn + Earth) Wednesdays during Capricorn and Saturdays during Gemini. Cheating on a loved one. A deceptive love affair. A dysfunctional marriage. Rape and taking advantage of someone sexually. A relationship based on jealousy and resentment. A relationship based only on sex. Intense sexual energy. Lust and unconventional sexual activity. Love expressed as a form of entropy. The disorder and chaos in a love relationship. A venereal disease. Sexual addiction and lust. The letters F O X are indicated. These two cards are strongly linked through numerology as the Lovers = 6 = 15 = The Devil.

The Lovers (6) + The Tower (16)

Gemini (Mercury + Air) + Mars Tuesdays during Gemini. A marriage that falls suddenly into ruin. The arguments and fights of a married couple. Loss of love or the destruction of a marriage. An unexpected love affair. An intense love affair. Destructive thoughts. Confusion in a marriage. Pain and pleasure. The pain that comes from lost love. Dangerous partnerships. A love affair that causes pain. An aggressive sex act or a rape. A cheating spouse. The moment of climax in a sexual relationship. Wireless communication. Radio waves and the electromagnetic spectrum. Cell phones. An angry phone call. The letters F O X G P Y are indicated.

The Lovers (6) + The Star (17)

Gemini (Mercury + Air) + Aquarius (Saturn + Air) Wednesdays during Aquarius and Saturdays during Gemini. A marriage that lasts a long time. Soulmates. Favorable unions. A long distance love relationship. A love song. Things that are heard. Things that travel through the air. Whispers and kind words that are spoken by lovers. Thoughts that can transcend time and space. The ability to understand the perspective of a lover. The letters F O X H Q Z are indicated. These two cards are strongly linked through the Air element. They are weakly linked through numerology since the Star = 17 = 8 = Mercury = Gemini = Lovers.

The Lovers (6) + The Moon (18)

Gemini (Mercury + Air) + Pisces (Jupiter + Water) Thursdays during Gemini and Wednesdays during Pisces. A deceptive lover. Perceptions that affect the emotions. Creative ideas. Plans and blueprints. Love relationships that blossom at night, around the time period of the full moon. Thinking carefully about dreams and intuition. Visions of the future. Emotional communication. Love relationships that move through cycles of hot and cold. Be cautious of new love relationships. A relationship with spiritual ties. A spiritually heightened sense of awareness during sex. An emotional outlet during sex. Orgasm. Chemists and chemical engineers. The letters F O X I R are indicated.

The Lovers (6) + The Sun (19)

Gemini (Mercury + Air) + The Sun Sundays during Gemini. A happy and successful relationship or marriage. A productive union. Abundance and success. Knowledge and understanding. Intellectual healing. Knowledge that leads to healing. Strong mental powers and the ability to solve difficult problems. The blessings of a newborn baby to a newly wedded couple. Being in love with your true soul mate. The letters F O X A J S are indicated. These two cards are weakly linked through numerology as the Lovers card = 6 = Sun = The Sun.

The Lovers (6) + Judgement (20)

Gemini (Mercury + Air) + Fire Behaviors that are the result of intentional thought. Forgiveness in a love relationship. A partnership that is renewed. Passion, understanding and transformation through communication. A love relationship is transformed. Love that is eternal. Someone who is still in love with someone who has passed away. The ghosts of the dead brought back to life through love. Communicating with the spirit of a loved one who has passed away. The letters F O X B K T are indicated.

The Lovers (6) + The World (21)

Gemini (Mercury + Air) + Saturn Saturdays during Gemini. A love relationship that develops slowly. A love relationship that starts at an old age. A long distance love affair. A couple that has a large age difference. Finding your soul mater after a long search. A loved one who is far away. Cultural differences that may cause obstacles in a love relationship. Thinking about something for a long time. Wisdom that stands the test of time. A rewarding relationship. A successful union. A couple that has been married for a long time. The practical side of marriage and relationships. Shared assets. A marriage license. The letters F O X C L U are indicated.

The Chariot (7) + Strength (8)

Cancer (Moon + Water) + Leo (Sun + Fire) Mondays during Leo and Sundays during Cancer. It is the Sun and the Moon. It can point to an eclipse. Travel may be needed for success. You will have a successful trip. It can be an ambulance as the Strength card can point to healing. It is freedom and responsibilities that are growing. Emotions are balanced through reason and the powers of the intuition are growing. It can be travel for the purpose of spiritual rejuvenation. The Cusp of Cancer and Leo (July 21st) is indicated. The fire of the Strength card fuels the Chariot. An ambulance or very fast, powerful car. The summer solstice. The letters G P Y H Q Z are indicated.

The Chariot (7) + The Hermit (9)

Cancer (Moon + Water) + Virgo (Mercury + Earth) Mondays during Virgo and Wednesdays during Cancer. Traveling alone. Emotions that affect behavior and thought. Travel to seek wisdom. Soul-searching that leads to progress. A skillful driver. A wise guide. A very good auto mechanic. A very old car. A very active old man who likes to travel. Wisdom that is gained through travel. An auto mechanic or engineer. A designer of cars, planes and trains. Travel alone for work or study. The letters G P Y I R are indicated. These two cards are weakly linked through numerology. The Hermit = 9 = Moon = Cancer = The Chariot.

The Chariot (7) + The Wheel of Fortune (10)

Cancer (Moon + Water) + Jupiter Thursdays during Cancer. A trip that leads to riches and good fortune. Winning a car or a trip in a contest. Psychic energy. Protective magic. The use of imagery and imagination before taking action. The Wheel of Fortune spins on the Chariot. The Wheel of Fortune (karma) is the engine that drives the chariot (the soul). The Chariot is the vehicle of self. The Wheel of Fortune is the cycle of life, death and rebirth. It is the development of the child in the womb. Take a journey to create new opportunities. Reflections of good fortune. The ripple effect of a good deed. The letters G P Y A J S are indicated.

The Chariot (7) + Justice (11)

Cancer (Moon + Water) + Libra (Venus + Air) Mondays during Libra and Fridays during Cancer. Traffic tickets. Going to court because of a car. Traveling with a lawyer. Balanced progress. Legal progress. Travel because of a court date. A song that is stuck in your head. Artistic inspiration. Balanced patterns of behavior. Spiritual progress as the result of karma. Songs or artwork that affects the emotions. Airplanes and astronauts. The letters G P Y B K T are indicated. These two cards are weakly linked through numerology as the Chariot = 7 = Venus = Libra = Justice.

The Chariot (7) + The Hanged Man (12)

Cancer (Moon + Water) + Water Amusement. Floods and rain. Perception affected by emotion. Diffraction and reflection of light in water. Sacrifice that leads to spiritual progress. Baptism. Travel over water. Travel by boat or over water. Driving in the rain. Swimming. A trip that gets cancelled. Restricted movement and discontinued progress. A rainy night. Cycles of emotion. A calm person. An inactive person. A passenger in a car. Following the crowd. Emotional dreams. Using water to see visions. Invisible currents that move through the water. Magnetism. Water pipes and plumbing. Canals and rivers. The letters G PY C L U are indicated. These two cards are strongly linked through the element of Water.

The Chariot (7) + Death (13)

Cancer (Moon + Water) + Scorpio (Mars + Water). Mondays during Scorpio and Tuesdays during Cancer. A dangerous, fatal car accident. A car that breaks down. Descent into the unconscious mind. Travel that leads to a change in perspective. Contact with ghosts and spirit. Astral travel. Going to a cemetery. A spiritual medium. A vehicle for a spiritual entity, like possession. Destructive travel. Negative psychic energy or power. A death spell. A spiritual exercise. A spiritual journey that uses a technology and involves death. A learning process that changes you. Learning a new language. The letters G PY D MV are indicated. These two cards are linked strongly through the element of Water.

The Chariot (7) + Temperance (14)

Cancer (Moon + Water) + Sagittarius (Jupiter + Fire) Mondays during Sagittarius and Thursdays during Cancer. Travel that leads to positive spiritual rewards. A spiritual pilgrimage. Blessings and protection during travel. A positive trip. Activities based on intuition. Progress made as the result of restraint. Taking someone else to a new place. A spirit guide. Spiritual travel. Welcoming strangers or travelers into your home. A missionary who travels to a faraway land. Traveling for religious or spiritual reasons. Voyages, especially be water. Washing things and purifying things with water. The letters G P Y E N W are indicated.

The Chariot (7) + The Devil (15)

Cancer (Moon + Water) + Capricorn (Saturn + Earth) Saturdays during Cancer and Mondays during Capricorn. Using transportation in an evil way. Going to an evil place. Demons attacking the soul. Confusion and being lost. A broken down car. Spiritual laziness. Not wanting to travel. A trip that is delayed due to financial problems. Progress that is blocked by jealousy or selfishness. Anger while travelling. Evil forces that travel in the soul. Negative spiritual energies. Using the emotions to time travel and manifest objects from the past or future. The use of a car for evil purposes. A car thief. The letters G P Y F O X are indicated.

The Chariot (7) + The Tower (16)

Cancer (Moon + Water) + Mars Tuesdays during Cancer. Don't travel, there is danger. Problems with a car. A car accident or car fire. A vehicle of war, a tank or army jeep. A conquering army. Motion and invasions. Reflection and the use of intuition to solve a competitive problem. Trying to anticipate the intentions of your enemies Driving fast and angry. Road rage! Loss of transportation. A bad trip or journey. A miserable journey. Problems while traveling. Unexpected problems with a car. Mental stress. A dangerous road. A cars electrical system. The letters G P Y are indicated. These two cards are strongly linked through numerology since The Chariot = 7 = 16 = The Tower.

The Chariot (7) + The Star (17)

Cancer (Moon + Water) + Aquarius (Saturn + Air). Mondays during Aquarius and Saturdays during Cancer. It is recurring dreams. These are feelings and thoughts that you have had for a long time. It may be someone that you fell in love with years ago or someone that you remember. You had a strong emotional connection to this person. It is feelings that blind your thoughts. You will connect to the spirit world through intense emotions. It is the influence of an old soul. It is also a card of travel. It may take a trip to find some new opportunity. It is time to explore. It is tears of happiness. A spaceship. Self-contemplation. The letters G P Y H Q Z are indicated.

The Chariot (7) + The Moon (18)

Cancer (Moon + Water) + Pisces (Jupiter + Water). Mondays during Pisces and Thursdays during Cancer. Astral travel through the deep subconscious mind, where angels fear to tread. A revelatory vision from beyond. Following your intuition. Travelling at night. A dream that solves an emotional problem. The Chariot represents the journey of the moon across the night sky. A trip by boat. Intuitive control of emotions: Compassion. The reproductive system. Generosity. Joy. Anticipation. Bliss. Using the emotions to access intuition. The ability to bring yourself to a highly emotional state in order to achieve something constructive. Emotional pilgrimage. Undersea exploration. Submarines and spaceships that travel to the moon. The Space shuttle. The letters G PY I R are indicated. These two cards are strongly linked through the Water element. They are weakly linked through numerology as the Moon = 18 = 9 = Moon = Cancer = Chariot.

The Chariot (7) + The Sun (19)

Cancer (Moon + Water) + The Sun Sundays during Cancer. A vacation. Travel for health reasons. Travel that leads to opportunity. Spending time in warm climates. Forward progress in spiritual matters. An eclipse. When the conscious and unconscious minds are in harmony. The ability to understand or control the dreams. Taking a trip to help others. A rewarding change and successful journey. A positive person who is well-liked and well-traveled. A lucky person with many skills, gifts and talents. The flight of Icarus. A limousine. A show off driving a fancy car. A vacation, holiday or travelling during the day. The letters G P Y A J S are indicated.

The Chariot (7) + Judgement (20)

Cancer (Moon + Water) + Fire. Hot water. A hot rainy night. Travel to somewhere from your past, like to a cemetery. Spiritual travel. Behaviors that are affected by unconscious emotions that are ready to come out. Religious rituals. Bowing and kneeling. Using the body as a symbol of some religious nature. Can be someone with impulsive moods. Behaviors that are closely linked with the emotions. Spiritual behaviors, dances and activities. Spiritual rituals. Travel to a place from your past. A car that has been restored. New motivation for spiritual advancement. Noah's ark and Jonas whale. The letters G P Y B K T are indicated.

The Chariot (7) + The World (21)

Cancer (Moon + Water) + Saturn Saturdays during Cancer. Sleep and sleeping. The emotional component of manifestation. Frozen lakes and ponds. Ice skating. Bridges. A lunar calendar. A time traveler. A world traveler. Travel that leads to success. Reaching your destination. A long trip. The soul that travels through time and affects the emotions. Patterns of behavior. Staying on a regular schedule. A relocation that brings rewards and success. Someone who may be afraid of travel. Use the spiritual body and unconscious mind for time travel and manifestation. Travel is needed to reach your true long term life goal. Follow your spirit and it will lead to success. Plumbers. The letters G P Y C L U are indicated.

Strength (8) + The Hermit (9)

Leo (Sun + Fire) | Virgo (Mercury + Earth). Sundays during Virgo and Wednesdays during Leo. The healing aspect of knowledge. Learning new healing techniques. Medical school. Morality. Self-mastery. Self-knowledge. Physical growth and the growth of knowledge. Retreats from society in order to heal. Vacation for rejuvenation. Meditation that leads to enlightenment. Asceticism. Conquering addiction through knowledge. A Buddhist monk. Vow of silence. Thought before action. Self-control leads to wisdom. Transformation of the physical through knowledge alone, not from others. Longevity, strong self-control and self-respect. The Cusp of Leo / Virgo (August 21st) is indicated. Food and nourishment for the body. Vitamins. Any kind of game that uses strategy. The letters H Q Z I R are indicated. These two cards are weakly linked through numerology since the Strength card = 8 = Mercury = Virgo = Hermit.

Strength (8) + The Wheel of Fortune (10)

Leo (Sun + Fire) + Jupiter Thursdays during Leo are indicated. This is an incredibly positive combination. It points to blessings and good health. It is a strong protector. Self-control will lead to good karma and blessings. Powerful opportunities to change the future. When the four elements are balanced, strength and power are the result. Exercise and creative healing activities are indicated. Taking the higher road will lead to riches beyond your wildest dreams. The power of destiny. Speculation, especially the stock market. The letters H Q Z A J S are indicated.

Strength (8) + Justice (11)

Leo (Sun + Fire) + Libra (Venus + Air) Sundays during Libra and Fridays during Leo. Holding out for what is right. Going against the crowd and standing up for justice. Generosity and helping others. Standing up for the truth. Doing the right thing. A balanced person. The power of the courts. A balanced force. Uplifting and motivating art or music. Forced kindness. Someone who is forced into charity or community service. Good health as the result of a balanced lifestyle. Art and music that leads to good health. A focus on needs, not wants. Creativity constrained by reason. The letters H Q Z B K T are indicated.

Strength (8) + The Hanged Man (12)

Leo (Sun + Fire) + Water. Charging up a battery. It could be a battery that ran down. The emotion of empathy. The motion in the water heats it up. Liquids that glow in the dark or give off light and heat. It is heat trapped within liquids. Sunlight warms the water. It is healing water. Self-control. Swimming underwater. Rainbows. Stored up energy. Discipline and Sacrifice will bring blessings. Sunlight reflected off of a lake. Light is bent as it travels through water. It is diffraction. It is a liquid that gives off light. Light travels through water. Convection currents in the ocean. This is holy water. This combination can also represent hot boiling water used for cooking. The letters H Q Z C L U are indicated.

Strength (8) + Death (13)

Leo (Sun + Fire) + Scorpio (Mars + Water) Sundays during Scorpio and Tuesdays during Leo. The ability to conquer death. Surviving a near-death experience. A serious disease. Vitality that is lost. Weakness and the loss of motivation. A strong powerful person who may be a killer. Someone who does not express their true intentions. Self-preservation. A very active person who may not care how their actions affect others. Self-control that leads to spiritual transformation. Someone who shows inner strength after the death of a loved one. Blood or blood poisoning. The letters H Q Z D M V are indicated.

Strength (8) + Temperance (14)

Leo (Sun + Fire) + Sagittarius (Jupiter + Fire) Thursdays during Leo and Sundays during Sagittarius. Strength through balance. Morality. Energy that is controlled. Restraint of force. This combination is good for matters of health. This is faith-healing and prayers for healing. The influence of the angels. Positive and constructive behavioral growth. Doing good deeds. Creative activities. Exercising for health reasons. A fireplace. A hospital. Self-control and moderation brings blessings. A religious or devoted person. Honey. The letters H Q Z E N W are indicated. These two cards are strongly connected through the element of Fire.

Strength (8) + The Devil (15)

Leo (Sun + Fire) + Capricorn (Saturn + Earth) Sundays during Capricorn and Saturdays during Leo. The ability to resist temptation. Being able to quit cold turkey. Conquering addictions and bad habits. Passing a spiritual test. Exercise and building up the physical body. A focus on the physical body. Self-gratification. Powerful energy and forceful violence. The struggle between good and evil. Heart disease. This combination can be a weak-minded person. Problems that must be solved. An enemy that must be conquered. The healing aspect of time. Activities that take a long time to complete. The letters H Q Z F O X are indicated. These two cards are weakly linked through numerology. The Devil = 15 = 6 = Sun = Leo = Strength.

Strength (8) + The Tower (16)

Leo (Sun + Fire) + Mars Tuesdays during Leo. A dangerous aggressive person. A strong competitive person. A destructive, powerful bomb. Trying to control yourself or someone else unsuccessfully. Electricity that can lead to healing. Rubies. Electrical energy. Destructive force. A conquering army. Swift, powerful and dangerous. A very intense person. A proud, active person who is not concerned with the opinions of others. Someone who may be impulsive. Taking action and asking questions later! A strong, but impulsive competitor. Explosions and fireworks. The letters H Q Z G P Y are indicated.

Strength (8) + The Star (17)

Leo (Sun + Fire) + Aquarius (Saturn + Air) Sundays during Aquarius and Saturdays during Leo. Inspiration and self-mastery. Self-control that leads to inspiration. Taking a long term view. Good health and longevity. A bright fire. It is the speed of light. When you see the stars in the sky, you are looking backward in time. A star is also a sun that is far away. These are long range effects of actions through space and time. This is the limit of the speed of light. Light = Time. The energy of destiny. Powerful opportunities. Time heals all wounds. A positive shift in perspective. Creative self-expression. How time and experience cause thought changes and behavioral changes. The letters H Q Z are indicated. These two cards are strongly linked through numerology since Strength = 8 = 17 = The Star.

Strength (8) + The Moon (19)

Leo (Sun + Fire) + Pisces (Jupiter + Water) Sundays during Pisces and Thursdays during Leo. Be cautious around powerful people. The water element can bring healing. Take action at night in matters of healing. Look for a day when the sun and moon are in the sky together. Patterns of behavior that make you stronger. Lifting weights or working out on a regular basis. Controlling the emotions through hypnosis or meditation. The healing power of moonlight. Gasoline and oil. Liquids that can be burned as fuel. Strong waves and tsunamis. Convection currents in water. The tides rushing in and out. The letters H Q Z I R are indicated.

Strength (8) + The Sun (19)

Leo (Sun + Fire) + The Sun. Sundays during Leo. This is fire. It is light, heat and energy. It is the healing energy of the Sun. It is a combination of power, gold and optimism. There will be opportunity and you will be strong enough to defeat your enemies. Truth will give you the power to triumph over your enemies. The color yellow will bring power. Large, feline animals. Good health and a strong, wealthy person. A famous person. Respect and the courage to do the right thing. Sunflowers. Motivation and the energy required to take advantage of an opportunity. The letters H Q Z A J S are indicated. These two cards are strongly linked through the Sun.

Strength (8) + Judgement (20)

Leo (Sun + Fire) + Fire A very hot day! Fire and sunburns. Controlling negative behaviors. Someone who is cautious about their behaviors. Heat and light that can lead to healing. Intentionally pulling oneself out of depression. Choosing to do the right thing. Power and energy that leads to change and renewal. Laser beams. The healing aspect of sunlight. A very social person. An entertainer or celebrity. A show off. Can be a very proud, active person. The energy released from fire. Ovens and stoves are also indicated. The letters H Q Z B K T are indicated. These two cards are strongly linked through the element of Fire.

Strength (8) + The World (21)

Leo (Sun | Fire) | Saturn Saturdays during Leo. The effect of time on behaviors and on healing. Self-control will lead you to your final goal. It is completion and final success after a struggle. Gold coins and money. The lion in the Strength card represents the animal or instinctual self. The World card points to the effects of time and experience on this animal self. The angel in the Strength card closes the jaws of the lion but will not hold it closed forever. Energy and power will be your successful reward. Behaviors should be controlled. Be careful how you behave in public. Show self-control to improve healing and reputation. Do not become too animalistic. Tap into your own higher self. Exercising the body for health reasons. This combination also represents a hot dry desert. Time heals all wounds. The letters H Q Z C L U are indicated.

The Hermit (9) + The Wheel of Fortune (10)

Virgo (Mercury + Earth) + Jupiter. Thursdays during Virgo. Purgatory. Isolation that leads to success. Self-examination. Someone who is defensive. Construction. Making plans to build or create something. The use of knowledge to create. An architect. Contemplating the future. Isolation brings change. Thinking about your destiny. Taking the 'big picture' approach. A skillful manager. Upper management. A busy person. Someone who is good at multi-tasking. A computer programmer. An accountant or financial planner. Stores and storekeepers. The letters I R A J S are indicated.

The Hermit (9) + Justice (11)

Virgo (Mercury + Earth) + Libra (Venus + Air) Wednesdays during Libra and Fridays during Virgo. Wisdom leads to balance. Intellectual property. Court cases involving science. A wise old lawyer. King Solomon a wise judge. Scientific art. Geometric or mathematically balanced art. The wisdom to carry out justice. Balanced thinking. A sequestered jury. Wisdom guides the execution of justice. The Cusp of Virgo / Libra (September 21st) is indicated. The Autumnal Equinox. Music is indicated. Balance brings wisdom. Pianos, violins and other stringed instruments. The letters I R B K T are indicated.

The Hermit (9) + The Hanged Man (12)

Virgo (Mercury + Earth) + Water The sacrifice of not interacting with society in order to spend time alone seeking knowledge. The emotions of shame or doubt. Examine the motivations for your actions. The ability to understand the emotional state of yourself and others. Acting on your faith. Meditation and focused thought. A spiritual teacher. Psychic abilities. The ability to affect matter with the emotions applied in a scientific way. A rainy Wednesday. Fasting. Cleansing of the physical body. The bowels and bowel trouble. Constipation. An emotional response to an object. The letters I R C L U are indicated.

The Hermit (9) + Death (13)

Virgo (Mercury + Earth) + Scorpio (Mars + Water) Wednesdays during Scorpio and Tuesdays during Virgo. The death of an old man. Spending time alone in mourning. Solitude and self-reflection that leads to transformation. Destructive thoughts. A negative or cynical person. Contemplation of destruction or loss. Someone who is feeling sorry for themselves. A person planning revenge on an enemy. Negative thoughts and wishing ill-will on someone. Someone unable to handle the pressures of life. Escapism. Secrets of every kind. An unsolved murder. The letters I R D M V are indicated.

The Hermit (9) + Temperance (14)

Virgo (Mercury + Earth) + Sagittarius (Jupiter + Fire). Wednesdays during Sagittarius and Thursdays during Virgo. Thought converted into action and implementation. The use of logic. The wise man calls upon the angels to act upon your prayers. This is a moment of spiritual revelation. It is an epiphany that leads to a constructive outcome. The solution to a problem is more likely spiritual or psychological rather than physical. Learning a skill. An apprentice who is not only learning how to make something, but is inspired to do so at a higher level. Psychotherapy or a physical therapist. Exercising to heal the body. A health regimen. Writers and writing. Solving a mathematical problem. Manufacturing. The actual behaviors that lead to manifestation. The letters I R E N W are indicated.

The Hermit (9) + The Devil (15)

Virgo (Mercury + Earth) + Capricorn (Saturn + Earth) Wednesdays during Capricorn and Saturdays during Virgo. Logic and time. Arcane arts, sciences, and alchemy. Logic of time dates and calendars. Dementia in old age. A mute or blind person. Body language. The use of sign language. Rituals using the body to make signs through motion. Giving somebody the finger. This combination is kinematics, or the study of body language. It is the behavior of culture. It is the study of chaos and confusion. It represents the gradual healing of the body. It can also be someone who is absent minded. Can be insanity or mental degradation with age. The loss of memories and logic. Forgetfulness and confusion. The letters I R F O X are indicated. These two cards are strongly linked through the element of Earth.

The Hermit (9) + The Tower (16)

Virgo (Mercury + Earth) + Mars Tuesdays during Virgo. Downfall and ruin that leads to solitude. Someone who pulls away from society due to negative circumstances. The wisdom to sense when danger is coming. An intelligent, but aggressive person who likes to argue. A sudden revelation of knowledge and insight. Science as a weapon of war. Dangerous technology. Codes and hidden communications that hide secret messages in times of war. A battle of wills. An electrician or electrical engineer. This can also be a military doctor. The letters I R G P Y are indicated.

The Hermit (9) + The Star (17)

Virgo (Mercury + Earth) + Aquarius (Saturn + Air) Wednesdays during Aquarius and Saturdays during Virgo. A period of grieving. A widower. A lonely old man. Spending time alone in quiet contemplation. A vow of silence. Reflecting on new opportunities. A problem that takes a long time to solve. Someone who prefers to be alone. An anti-social person. Astrologers and prophets. People who are outcast from society. People who study psychology and human behavior. The letters I R H Q Z are indicated. These two cards are weakly linked through numerology. The Star = 17 = 8 = Mercury = Virgo = Hermit.

The Hermit (9) + The Moon (18)

Virgo (Mercury + Earth) + Cancer (Jupiter + Water) Thursdays during Virgo and Wednesdays during Cancer are indicated as times of action. Take action at night. Spend time alone at night under the light of the moon. The moonlight brings wisdom. Pay attention to dreams. The wise use of psychic energy. Hallucinations, visions and dreams. Symbolic dreams and visions. Gazing into the crystal ball. Manifestations that come from the emotions. Build in a mathematical or geometric way. A suspicious scientist. A wise man who is a recluse. A spiritual guide that visits your dreams. A psychologist or psychoanalyst. This combination is the use of hypnosis. Retirement. The letters I and R are indicated. These two cards are weakly linked through numerology. The Hermit = 9 = 18 = Moon.

The Hermit (9) + The Sun (19)

Virgo (Mercury + Earth) + The Sun Sundays during Virgo. Isolation that brings happiness and spiritual revelation. This combination is positive for healing. Successful treatment of a disease. An older person who is very healthy. Productive thinking. A wealthy, successful, wise man. A generous person. Someone who has accomplished their life goal and is enjoying the rewards of success. Bees, honey and beekeepers. Clothing. Chemists and biochemists. Evolution and the study of DNA. People will seek you out for the knowledge you have. The letters I R A J S are indicated.

The Hermit (9) + Judgement (20)

Virgo (Mercury + Earth) + Fire Using skill and knowledge to solve a difficult problem. Solitude and reflection that leads to self-transformation. A wise man with the power to forgive. Meditation that leads to self-awareness and understanding. Fasting and spiritual revelation. Can be a combination of physical illness or weakness. Neglecting physical needs for the sake of spiritual pursuits. A very motivated person who neglects food or sleep. Someone who is not taking care of the physical body. A scientific experiment. Things that are purified by fire. The letters I R B K T are indicated.

The Hermit (9) + The World (21)

Virgo (Mercury + Earth) + Saturn. Saturdays during Virgo. The time involved in the manifestation of something. The passage of time changes as we age. Taking stock of the product of a long-term process of creation, The sculptor standing at a distance from his work to determine his next move. A clock, a calendar, a birthday, an anniversary. Time represented by numbers. Matter creates time, because time is motion, and motion is predicated on matter. The wisdom from a long life, or the growth of knowledge over time. Experience. A wise old successful businessman. Offices and office workers. Celibacy. Someone who is paid by the hour. A time clock. The letters I R C L U are indicated.

The Wheel of Fortune (10) + Justice (11)

Jupiter + Libra (Venus + Air) Thursdays during Libra. Constructive, artistic thoughts. Intentional relationships. Beneficial legal documents. An order of protection. A positive decision from the courts. A large legal settlement. A balanced destiny. A balanced opportunity. A future that is in the hands of the courts. Good luck and good karma. Taking a balanced approach to life. The four elements in perfect balance. The male-female, dualistic aspect of life. A well balanced person. Understanding the perspective of a loved one. The laws of karma. The letters A J S B K T are indicated.

The Wheel of Fortune (10) + The Hanged Man (12)

Jupiter + Water Very beneficial. Happiness. It can be a spectator in the game of life. It is a passive person. It is a positive constructive emotional state. A rainy Thursday. Constructive emotions. Self-confidence. Humble and generous. Peace and protection. It is time for swimming. The cycle of life has been suspended. An opportunity has been discontinued. Choices may be limited. Water is a passive element, so sit back and let the blessings fall into your lap. This is the sign of a good loser and a good winner. A prayer for protection. The color blue will be important. Baptism and holy water. The body depends on water for life. Water gives life which spins the wheel of karma. Only life can create karma. The emotional response to karma. Only when something makes a choice does it have life. Doing charity work. The letters A J S C L U are indicated.

The Wheel of Fortune (10) + Death (13)

Jupiter + Scorpio (Mars + Water). Thursdays during Scorpio. Generally a fortunate combination, that is spiritually positive. The Wheel is the four elements, which combined with death point to spiritual evolution. Fateful transformation. Loss in a game of chance, but for the greater good. Hitting rock bottom before recovery. A tragedy that occurs that motivates one to change the world. Reincarnation. Intense emotional motivation. A beautiful grave or tomb. Tax collectors. Money that is lost due to speculation. The letters A J S D M V are indicated. These two cards are weakly linked through numerology. The Death card = 13 = 4 = Jupiter = Wheel of Fortune.

The Wheel of Fortune (10) + Temperance (14)

Jupiter + Sagittarius (Jupiter + Fire) Thursdays during Sagittarius. Self-preservation. Acting in self-defense. Constructive actions. Prayers will bring blessings. You will receive good karma and visits from the angels. Your prayers will be answered and great fortune will fall into your lap. Your future and destiny are balanced. Take a moderate approach for success. A creative person. Foundation building behaviors. The ability to follow a business plan to a successful conclusion. The ability to motivate others to create positive things for society. Abundance. Activities designed to raise money for those in need. Charities. Banks and banking. The letters A J S E N W are indicated. These two cards are strongly linked through the planet Jupiter.

The Wheel of Fortune (10) + The Devil (15)

Jupiter + Capricorn (Saturn + Earth) Thursdays during Capricorn. It represents slow changes to the physical body. It can be conquering disease or addiction. It is the aging process. It can point to illness in the physical body that may be the result of karma. It can point to bodybuilding or growing. It is old age. It takes time for ideas and plans to be created and built. A project will take a long time to complete. It is the ability to save money. It is holding on to objects from the past. Valuable things that may be very old. It is creating or building something that will last a long time. Buying and selling. Charging interest on a loan. Being in debt. The letters A J S F O X are indicated.

The Wheel of Fortune (10) + The Tower (16)

Jupiter + Mars Offense and defense. Unexpected good fortune. A good opportunity that is suddenly destroyed. Gambling on the outcome of a sporting event. A standoff in a war. The interplay between constructive and destructive forces. A strong defense and a strong offense. This combination can be unexpected bad karma or destiny that has been dramatically changed suddenly. The loss of opportunity and a destructive future. It can also be protection from harm or protection from a dangerous person or situation. An intense, important situation. A life-changing event. The random nature of karma. Things that seem unpredictable or unrelated. The letters A J S G P Y are indicated.

The Wheel of Fortune (10) + The Star (17)

Jupiter + Aquarius (Saturn + Air) Thursdays during Aquarius. Hope for the future. Faith that good luck is coming. Favorable changes and hopeful opportunities. Someone who analyzes the causes and effects of their own behavior. The effects of karma on thought. The effect of time on thought and self-improvement. A long range view of life. The spinning of the wheel of fortune is caused by thought. It is randomness and unexpected events that change the course of your life. It is karma and destiny affected by thought. Self-analysis through the balance of the four elements. The letters A J S H Q Z are indicated.

The Wheel of Fortune (10) + The Moon (18)

Jupiter + Pisces (Jupiter + Water) Thursdays during Pisces. The constructive use of water. Swimming pools. A moat around a castle. Water used as a defense. The natural rhythm of karma. Cycles of positive and negative emotions. The lunar cycle. Constructive emotions. An obscure destiny. Be wary of new opportunity. Be careful to not be deceived. Good luck at night. The use of the emotions to manipulate people. False tears that cause guilt. Hiding your true intentions from others. Charitable organizations. The letters A J S I R are indicated. These two cards are linked strongly through the planet Jupiter.

The Wheel of Fortune (10) + The Sun (19)

Jupiter + The Sun A very successful destiny. A productive change. A rewarding future. This is a very positive combination of two very positive planetary forces! Gold and prosperity! Winning the lottery! Everything will work out. It is receiving your good karma. Great riches and wealth. Good health and protection. Great unexpected blessings. All the blessings of health and wealth. Being blessed and protected. Success and victory. The center of things. The center of the wheel is motionless. The planets revolve around the Sun. This combination is focused energy. The letters A J S are indicated. These two cards are strongly linked through numerology. The Sun = 19 = 10 = Wheel of Fortune.

The Wheel of Fortune (10) + Judgement (20)

Jupiter + Fire Constructive activities. Being judged by your actions. Forgiveness and redemption. Enthusiasm. The spinning wheel of destiny gives off energy in the form of light and heat. Karma that is readjusted through forgiveness. DNA is affected by karma. The random nature of heredity and genetics. The child that is born is the result of the genetic karma of the parents. Reincarnation is necessary to rebalance karma. An altered future. Protective behaviors. A strong guardian. The use of fire for protection. The constructive use of fire. A fireplace. A heater. A cooking stove. This combination is the judgement of the soul of man based on our deeds and thoughts. The letters A J S B K T are indicated.

The Wheel of Fortune (10) + The World (21)

Jupiter + Saturn. Thursdays and Saturdays are indicated. Karma creates time. Karma moves through time and space. Karma is not balanced instantly. There is a time lag between cause and effect. The colors are blue and black. The Wheel of Fortune is karma and the laws of cause and effect. The World card is time. The Wheel spins and so does the World. We will reach our long term goals. Time travel can bring good luck. There is good fortune and success after a struggle. All results of karma are distributed through time and space. Even things with a low probability of happening will still happen eventually. Yes, people do win the lottery! Luck is a function of time and timing. The letters A J S C L U are indicated.

Justice (11) + The Hanged Man (12)

Libra (Venus + Air) + Water Emotional balance. Contentment. Music that draws an emotional response. Emotions that are understood. Taking the blame for someone else's mistakes. Covering up for someone. Justice is not given. There is a delay in punishing the guilty. The Hanged Man has been found guilty by the courts. A legal matter will be dropped or dismissed. On overly emotional person. Someone who understands and contemplates their own emotions. An artist or musician. A glass of champagne. The letters B K T C L U are indicated.

Justice (11) + Death (13)

Libra (Venus + Air) + Scorpio (Mars + Water) Fridays during Scorpio and Tuesdays during Libra. It is the death penalty. The decision of the court is death. It is transformation. Self-analysis of the emotions. There is a perfect balance between the male / female aspect of the soul during death. The soul that lives on after death has no gender. Only in life and the creation of karma, do we have existence split into the sexes of male and female. Balance is necessary in order to contemplate the realm of the spirit. Death is a part of life and holds a certain beauty. Sometimes death is the result of karma. Contact with the spirit world will bring balance. The cusp of Libra / Scorpio (October 21st) is indicated. Disease like diabetes and asthma. The letters B K T D M V are indicated.

Justice (11) + Temperance (14)

Libra (Venus + Air) + Sagittarius (Jupiter + Fire) Fridays during Sagittarius and Thursdays during Libra. A very balanced combination. The balance of art and science. The balance of logic and emotion. Angelic judgement, probably a blessing. Left and right side of brain. The internal union of opposites. A fortunate outcome to a court case. Trials and lawyers. A public defender. Legal arbitration. A female airline hostess. Wills and other legal documents. Insurance policies. A confident talented person. Someone with special talents or gifts. Courting. The letters B K T E N W are indicated.

Justice (11) + The Devil (15)

Libra (Venus + Air) + Capricorn (Saturn + Earth) Fridays during Capricorn and Saturdays during Libra. A legal matter that causes anger or resentment. It can point to divorce due to adultery. Evil thoughts and lusting after a married woman or man. An unjust situation based on lies. A criminal that is set free based on lies or a technicality. Someone who bears false witness in court. The punishment of criminals by the courts. Lust and sexual obsessions. Sculptures and art are indicated. Old paintings or songs. Flutes or other wind instruments. The beauty of the physical body. The use of scales or balances. Jails and jailors. Flies and spiders. Insects and mosquitoes. Bats. The letters B K T F O X are indicated.

Justice (11) + The Tower (16)

Libra (Venus + Air) + Mars Tuesdays during Libra. A bad legal decision. Disaster in the courtroom. Arguments. A surprise witness that sends the accused to the electric chair! The union of male and female. Unexpected, unpredictable decision from the courts. Electrical energy that is balanced and controlled. Receiving bad karma. Loss and ruin as the result of a court decision. It can be someone who turns their life around after being punished. The thoughts involved when interacting with a loved one. The letters B K T G P Y are indicated. These two cards are weakly linked through numerology. The Tower = 16 = 7 = Venus = Libra= Justice.

Justice (11) + The Star (17)

Libra (Venus + Air) + Aquarius (Saturn + Air) Saturdays during Libra and Fridays during Aquarius. The decision of the court is favorable. Having a balanced perspective. Spending time thinking about love from the past or future. Time travel using thought. Art, color and music are indicated. A windy day. Successful treatment of a mental disorder. A comedian or witty cynic. The breath of life. How your perception of love changes over time. The letters B K T H Q Z are indicated. These two cards are linked strongly through the element of Air.

Justice (11) + The Moon (18)

Libra (Venus + Air) + Pisces (Jupiter + Water) Thursdays during Libra and Fridays during Pisces are indicated. The time period of the full moon is indicated. The interplay between reason and compassion. This is someone who is intuitive and practical. Activity at night. Balance will be restored. Court cases will be settled near the full moon. It is a time of love and peace. Positive perceptions lead to happy emotions. Beware of deception in a court of law. Be sure to read the fine print. The use of psychic energy to rebalance karma or to speed up or slow down the effects of karma. It represents balanced cycles of nature and points to beautiful music. Music played under the moonlight. Beautiful fountains made of copper and stone. Photographs and photographers. The letters B K T I R are indicated.

Justice (11) + The Sun (19)

Libra (Venus + Air) + The Sun Sundays during Libra. Creative and artistic thoughts. Optimistic balanced thoughts. A natural artist. Beauty and ones response to beauty. Lemons and limes. Success and gold. The power of positive thinking. A positive legal settlement. Balance is required for healing. Happiness and equality. A very positive legal success. A very intelligent person. Wisdom. Bringing out the truth in a legal matter. New creative ideas. Beautiful art and music. The Equinox. A warm breeze. Balance brings happiness. Happiness leads to balance. The letters B K T A J S are indicated.

Justice (11) + Judgement (20)

Libra (Venus + Air) + Fire. The verdict, the decision of the court. Karma. Balanced and fair behaviors. Reincarnation as a chance to rebalance karma. Actions that affect karma. The resurrection of the dead to be judged. Dance and choreography. Ritual dance. Trial by fire. You will be judged by your actions. Something from the past will be brought back to life. Actions that are motivated by love. The courts showing mercy and granting forgiveness. A new life being given. A second chance. Magnetism. Balance and equilibrium. The air fuels the fire. A hot wind. Windmills and energy generated from the wind. The letters B K T are indicated. These two cards are strongly linked through numerology. The Justice card = 11 = 20 = Judgement.

Justice (11) + The World (21)

Libra (Venus + Air) + Saturn Saturdays during Libra. Holding a balanced thought for a long time. Training the mind to be balanced. The way thoughts about a love relationship change over time. The beauty of nature. A marriage that lasts a long time. A legal matter that comes to a conclusion after a long time period. Legal decisions that are delayed. Balanced financial success. A successful legal decision. Ideas that are made manifest through art or music. The importance of balanced thought in manifestation. The use of balances and gravity. Making measurements of physical phenomena. Balance is required to complete a complicated task. The colors black and green are indicated. Taxes and tax collectors. The letters B K T C L U are indicated.

The Hanged Man (12) + Death (13)

Water + Scorpio (Mars + Water) Mourning the loss of a loved one. Tears of sadness and loss. Drowning. Dangerous floods and water. Can be very hot water. War at sea. Transformations that are stopped. Things that come to a complete end. Emotional closure. Giving your life to save another. Giving up a bad habit. Violent storms and tsunamis. Liquids that cause death for example alcohol or poisons. Can also point to urine or stomach acid. Can be stagnant pools of water. The letters C L U D M V are indicated. These two cards are strongly linked through the element of Water.

The Hanged Man (12) + Temperance (14)

Water + Sagittarius (Jupiter + Fire). Emotional motivation behind action. Helping someone. Holy water. Purification of water by boiling it. Jupiter is beneficial. The emotion of trust. Spiritual blessings you will receive as the result of sacrifice. A spiritual pilgrimage. Offering your time to charity. Focus on the spiritual world. Doing good deeds that will lead to good karma. Communication with the angels through sacrifice. Tithing. Donating your time and energy to a charity. Protective energy. Taking the blame for someone else's mistake. Change of perspective brought about through a spiritual or angelic experience. Prophets. A life preserver. The letters C L U E N W are indicated.

The Hanged Man (12) + The Devil (15)

Water + Capricorn (Saturn + Earth) Laziness. Idleness. The emotion of fear. Selfishness. Negative, greedy emotions. Temptation. Deception. Allowing bad things to happen around you. A rainy Saturday. Anger and jealousy that is limited or ceased. The ability to give up bad habits and turn your back on sin. This is Christ paying the debt of sin for mankind. Suspicion and overindulgence. Physical pleasures that are the result of emotional triggers. Smoking, overeating, drinking or sexual issues. Cold water and ice. Poisoned water. The letters C L U F O X are indicated. These two cards are weakly linked through numerology. The Hanged Man = 12 = 3 = Saturn = Capricorn = The Devil.

The Hanged Man (12) + The Tower (16)

Water + Mars. Hot boiling water. Suicide. A suicide bomber taking action for emotional reasons. Anger and negative emotions that may be directed inward. Unpredictable emotions. The emotion of surprise. Dangerous water. Storms and hurricanes. Ruin and danger that is barely avoided. Unexpected emotional turmoil. A passive person that experiences an impulsive moment of emotional outburst. Someone who needs to release their emotional energy in a physical way. An emotionally competitive person. Passive aggressive energy. Using water as a weapon of war. Warfare at sea. The Navy. Dangerous submarines and torpedoes. The letters C L U G P Y are indicated.

The Hanged Man (12) + The Star (17)

Water + Aquarius (Saturn + Air) Procrastination. Being unhappy in your current situation. Depression, anxiety or worry. Reflection on mistakes made in your past. A limited perspective and limited opportunities. Someone facing emotional or mental pressure. Someone who does not focus on the present. An emotional time traveler. Someone with a delayed emotional response to a situation. Repressed stress. Bad timing and being late for an important appointment. A sad or cynical person. The letters C L U H Q Z are indicated. These two cards are weakly linked through numerology as The Hanged Man = 12 = 3 = Saturn = Aquarius = The Star.

The Hanged Man (12) + The Moon (18)

Water + Pisces (Jupiter + Water). Rainy Thursdays are indicated. Sacrifices are indicated. Constructive and generous emotions. The emotion of sadness or pity. This combination points to sympathy and understanding. Empathy. The time period of the full moon is indicated. Thursdays will be active. There is more activity at night. Give up the lesser good for the greater good. The Moon is sometimes used to measure time. There is a wave of energy, cycling between hot and cold. Normal cycles of behavior will be suspended. Can point to menopause. Swamps and boats are indicated. Also, things that dissolve like sugar or salt. Water wells are indicated. The delayed reaction between thought and emotion. Swimming pools or pools of water. The letters C L U I R are indicated. These two cards are strongly linked through the element of Water.

The Hanged Man (12) + The Sun (19)

Water + The Sun Warm water. Healing waters. The emotion of joy. Sacrificing your life for another. Positive emotional state. Anticipation. Happiness through suffering and sacrifice. Doing charity work for the less fortunate. Limited success and suspended happiness. Someone who is not using their talents or gifts effectively. Someone who has a hard time relaxing or having fun. Someone who is too serious. Life giving water or blood. The letters C L U A J S are indicated.

The Hanged Man (12) + Judgement (20)

Water + Fire This is love. The ability to forgive and make sacrifices for a loved one. It can be taking the blame for the actions of others. Two elements that are opposites. It is the yin and yang. It is the male and female, the positive and negative poles of the magnet. Fire is the behavior of man. Water is the emotions. Emotions motivate behaviors and behaviors create new emotions. Sacrifice and forgive. This is the crucifixion and resurrection of Christ. It is the holy spirit and the gift of baptism. This is a very powerful combination because it is the union of two pure elements. It represents the proton-electron interaction in the atom. The letters C L U B K T are indicated.

The Hanged Man (12) + The World (21)

Water + Saturn A rainy Saturday. Patience. The effect of time on the emotions. Sacrificing the lesser good for the greater good. Plans that are changed at the last minute. Limited success. A life-changing experience. Knowledge that comes from personal experience. The ability to prioritize your life and get the 'big picture' view of life. Waterfalls and the effects of gravity on water. Currents in large bodies of water. The formation of ice crystals and snowflakes. This combination represents things that are stable, but stagnant. It can represent the flooding of the Earth. It represents success that may be suspended, delayed or abandoned. The letters C L U are indicated. These two cards are strongly linked through numerology as The Hanged Man = 12 = 21 = The World.

Death (13) + Temperance (14)

Scorpio (Mars + Water) + Sagittarius (Jupiter + Fire) Tuesdays during Sagittarius and Thursdays during Scorpio. Dramatic change. Prayers for the dead. The Angel of death. The destruction of the creative process. Giving up. Behaviors that are affected by emotions. Prayers will end mourning. A guardian angel that will protect you from death. Spiritual forces that interact with angels. Prayers can bring the soul of a loved one to visit. Pay attention to messages from the body. Blood. It is the aging process. The cusp of Scorpio / Sagittarius (November 21st) is indicated. Become balanced to enter the spirit world. Sweat and evaporation. Hunters. The letters D MV E N W are indicated. These two cards are weakly linked through numerology as the Death card = 13 = 4 = Jupiter = Sagittarius = Temperance = 14 = 5 = Mars = Scorpio = Death.

Death (13) + The Devil (15)

Scorpio (Mars + Water) + Capricorn (Saturn + Earth) Tuesdays during Capricorn and Saturdays during Scorpio. A very scary combination. Disease. Illness. Mortality. Evil. The wages of sin is death. Time destroys the body and emotions. It is insanity and emotional self-loathing. It is addiction that leads to death. It is murder and evil. The end of a friendship due to anger and violence. Spiritual time travel. Self-destructive bad habits that cause damage to the body. Anger that is directed unconsciously towards the self. Smoking, drinking, and eating disorders. Mental illness as a result of sin and guilt. Someone who dies and is sent to Hell. Black magic and witchcraft. Cemeteries. The letters D M V F O X are indicated.

Death (13) + The Tower (16)

Scorpio (Mars + Water) + Mars Tuesdays during Scorpio. Very dangerous. A tall building that is destroyed in an act of war. This is September 11th! Danger, death, and war. Violence anger and destruction that brings about revolution and emotional response. War that brings tears. It is the emotional response to death and violence. Unexpected tragedy. A horrible combination! Ruin and Loss. A violent, angry ghost. Spirits that use electricity to cause harm. Emotional aggression. Yelling and screaming at someone. Alcohol abuse. Making someone cry. Broken bones, cuts and bruises. The letters D M V G P Y are indicated. These two cards are strongly linked through planet Mars.

Death (13) + The Star (17)

Scorpio (Mars + Water) + Aquarius (Saturn + Air) Tuesdays during Aquarius and Saturdays during Scorpio. Time destroys perspective. Mental stress due to the death of a loved one. Confused perceptions can lead to anger or violence. It is post-traumatic stress. Giving up hope or losing faith. The end of an opportunity. Stars reflected in the water. When you look at a star, you are looking into the past. Memories from the past that evoke an emotional response. An image or picture of a loved one who has passed away. A delayed emotional response to an event. The circulation of blood. Toilets and sewer systems. The letters D M V H Q Z are indicated.

Death (13) + The Moon (18)

Scorpio (Mars + Water) + Pisces (Jupiter + Water) Thursdays during Scorpio and Tuesdays during Pisces. Mourning the loss of a loved one. An emotional response. Dreams of death. Dreams of the spirit world. Visions of ghosts and spiritual energies. Beware, there is a danger of death. A death at night, around the time period of the full moon. Someone who faces mental stress due to the death of a loved one. Pictures or images of the dead. Holy water. Baptism. Drowning. Visions and sensations. A ghost that visits your dreams. Astral travel. Reptiles, crabs and lobsters. Séances. The letters D M V I R are indicated. These two cards are strongly linked through the element of Water and weakly linked through numerology as the Dearth card = 13 = 4 = Jupiter = Pisces = Moon.

Death (13) + The Sun (19)

Scorpio (Mars + Water) + Sun Sundays during Scorpio. Death and rebirth. Reincarnation. Death is needed for the growth of the emotions. Learning love through loss. Growing emotionally due to the death of a loved one. A serious disease. Success and happiness comes to an end. The Death of the Sun happens during an eclipse. A newborn baby dies. An abortion. The release of the spirit at the moment of death. Blood carries the life force. Spiritual energy as opposed to matter. A near death experience that leads to spiritual rejuvenation. A famous, but tragic figure. Someone who dies at a young age. The letters D M V A J S are indicated.

Death (13) + Judgement (20)

Scorpio (Mars + Water) + Fire Negative emotions that lead to destructive behaviors. It is the death penalty. Death is the final judgement. This combination can point to resurrection. The dead are rising from the grave. Old ideas brought back to life. It can be the final decision of the court. The Death card points to the spirit world. The judgement card is forgiveness. Focus on life not death. It is the afterlife. This combination points to someone who cheated death or survived a serious illness. This can point to a vigilante. Someone who is killed by fire. Cremation of the body. Recycling. The letters D M V B K T are indicated.

Death (13) + The World (21)

Scorpio (Mars + Water) + Saturn Saturdays during Scorpio. The physical body will be left behind and return to the Earth after death. Death comes to all in time. This can be someone who builds up anger or another negative emotion over a long time period. Someone with anger problems. Success will come to an end. It is time to quit a job. Success is lost and destroyed. It can represent the Sabbath. The emotional strain of hard work. Long time periods of violence, anger and war. The death of the world. A freshly dug grave. A graveyard. Taxes and tax collectors. The clothing that a corpse will wear. The body is returned to the earth. Ashes to ashes, dust to dust. The letters D M V C L U are indicated.

Temperance (14) + The Devil (15)

Sagittarius (Jupiter + Fire) + Capricorn (Saturn + Earth) Thursdays during Capricorn and Saturdays during Sagittarius. The battle of good vs. evil. It is the angels and the demons. Prayer can conquer the evil of the devil. Restraining violence or selfishness. Sin can be controlled through balance and prayer. Protective prayers. Aliens. Old buildings or churches. A fortress. Old places where people gather. It is the cusp of Sagittarius / Capricorn (December 21st). It is the Winter Solstice. It is spiritual energy held in the fleshly body. The duality of existence. The casting out of demons. The letters E N W F O X are indicated.

Temperance (14) + The Tower (16)

Sagittarius (Jupiter + Fire) + Mars Tuesdays during Sagittarius. Unexpected blessings. An angel that suddenly appears. Prayers. Protection from an accident. Activation. Avoiding danger. Ammunition. Arrows. Sidestepping calamity. The ability to sense danger before it approaches. Times of trouble are suddenly over, so enjoy a moment of peace. A very active time period. Prayers that can call down the lightening. Sudden revelation as the result of prayer. Radio broadcasting. The letters E N W G P Y are indicated. These two cards are weakly linked through numerology. The Temperance card = 14 = 5 = Mars = The Tower.

Temperance (14) + The Star (17)

Sagittarius (Jupiter + Fire) + Aquarius (Saturn + Air) Thursdays during Aquarius and Saturdays during Sagittarius. Being in the right place at the right time. Hopes that have been restrained. It is a balanced destiny. A moderate perspective. Alternative prospects. Advertisement writers. The ability to control your own destiny. Prayers that should be prayed at the proper time. Feeling unaware or detached from reality. An altered state of mental awareness due to prayer. Meditation that leads to spiritual awakening. Mental confusion. Counselors. The letters E N W H Q Z are indicated.

Temperance (14) + The Moon (18)

Sagittarius (Jupiter + Fire) + Pisces (Jupiter + Water) Thursdays during Sagittarius and Pisces. Constructive behaviors motivated by emotion. Spirituality. Compassion for others that leads to charity work. Messages from the Angels that appear in dreams. Prayers that are spoken at night or near the time period of the full moon. Self-control will lead to mental stability. This combination can point to body language or unconscious methods of communication. The ability to control your dreams. Being conscious of visions. Psychic messages from the angels. An unconscious warning of impending danger. Dreams and dream consciousness. Lifeguards and swimming instructors. The use of holy water. The letters E N W I R are indicated. These two cards are strongly linked through the planet Jupiter.

Temperance (14) + The Sun (19)

Sagittarius (Jupiter + Fire) + Sun Sundays during Sagittarius. Prayers that bring healing. Prayers that bring fertility and abundance. Religious faith. Gold and success. Fire and light. Happiness and success as the result of moderation. Do not overdo it, and you will reap great rewards. A spiritual experience. A vision seen during the day. Someone who is holding back emotionally. Someone who may feel uncomfortable in social settings. Your higher mind. Your holy guardian angel. It is generosity and showing kindness to strangers. An excellent active combination. The letters E N W A J S are indicated.

Temperance (14) + Judgement (20)

Sagittarius (Jupiter + Fire) + Fire Very busy doing good works. Prayers bring transformation and positive behavioral change. Light and heat are indicated. Restraint and control will bring change and transformation. This is busy charity work. Someone in a heightened state of awareness due to physical overload. A battery that is fully charged. Ideas from the past brought back to life through balance and self-control. Resurrection. It is the ability to change your behavior through prayer and angelic intercession. An idea or activity from the past that is brought back to life will bring blessings. Prayer will bring the dead back to life. A near death experience. Spirituality. Fire that is used as protection. Fire used for light or heat. The letters E N W B K T are indicated. These two cards are strongly linked through the element of Fire.

Temperance (14) + The World (21)

Sagittarius (Jupiter + Fire) + Saturn Saturdays during Sagittarius. This combination represents constructive behavior. The ability to plan for the future. Hard work that leads to rewards, both material and spiritual. Prayers that will be answered. Angels that will influence matter. Behaviors that bring about manifestation. Plots of land. A monument or obelisk. A meeting that brings success. Blessings from the angels. Protection and assured success. Moderation and balance will bring success. The accomplishments of a life's work. Achievement and recognition. Banks and banking. The letters E N W C L U are indicated.

The Devil (15) + The Tower (16)

Capricorn (Saturn + Earth) + Mars Tuesdays during Capricorn. Time + Matter + Destruction. Erosion, the destructive aspects of time. Entropy, chaos, natural disorder. Anger. Aging, disease, and illness. Discipline + Purpose + Drive = Success. Temptation and anger. Fire, lust, and sin. The downfall of man. The fallen angels. Accidents. Unexpected temptation leading to downfall. The consequences of pride. Destructive consequences of a life devoted to sin. Unpredictable downfall, like a lightning strike from beyond. Bringing an end to a dark period, hitting rock bottom which leads to the potential for change. The downfall of man due to sin. The letters F O X G P Y are indicated.

The Devil (15) + The Star (17)

Capricorn (Saturn + Earth) + Aquarius (Saturn + Air) Saturdays during Capricorn and Aquarius are indicated. The cusp of Capricorn and Aquarius (January 21st) is indicated. Time is critical here. Proper timing of your actions will determine success or failure. This combination can point to mental illness, addictions or compulsions. It is someone who is hoping for the downfall of others. Trying to ruin the opportunities of others. Distance and time travel are indicated. First the mind must time travel, then matter will follow. Do not be tempted to give up on a dream just because it seems to take a long time to achieve. It is faith that conquers the devil. Triangles and the color black are indicated. A cold wind. The letters F O X H Q Z are indicated. These two cards are strongly linked through the planet Saturn.

The Devil (15) + The Moon (18)

Capricorn (Saturn I Earth) I Pisces (Jupiter + Water) Saturdays during Pisces and Thursdays during Capricorn are indicated. Addictions and compulsions. It is evil that comes into the dreams. Evil deeds and sin that have become patterns. This can be mountain rivers. Be cautious of selfishness. This can be paranoia or dreams of demons. It is spiritual dark forces. It is culture and long term patterns of behavior. It can be selfishness or narcissism. Do not fall in love with your own reflection. It is the ripple effect of an evil deed. Sin is reflective. Do not project your own darkness onto others. It is a moon shadow. It is the dark, waning moon. It points to the full moon time period in Capricorn. It is the instinct of self-preservation. The confusing aspect of dreams. Nightmares! Crystals and crystal formations. Drug users and smugglers. Ovarian cancer. The letters F O X I R are indicated.

The Devil (15) + The Sun (19)

Capricorn (Saturn + Earth) + Sun. Sundays during Capricorn are indicated. Conquering temptation. Material success and abundance. Investments, successful gold mining. Transmutation—turning lead into gold. Death and rebirth. Solar cell. Sun dial. The rewards of conquering temptation. A proud person. A showoff. A self-centered but generous person. A wasteful, but happy person. A desert. A hot dry place. Redemption. The resurrection of Christ that conquers sin. Fool's gold. Things that look beautiful or enticing on the outside, but are dark and evil on the inside. A hypocritical person. The letters F O X A J S are indicated. These two cards are weakly linked through numerology because the Devil = 15 = 6 = Sun.

The Devil (15) + Judgement (20)

Capricorn (Saturn + Earth) + Fire This can point to food and fancy dinners. This is evil behavior. It is giving in to temptation. Anger and jealousy that causes major upheavals. This is the judgement of sin. The fires of hell transforming the souls of the sinner. The effect of time on behavior. Earthly power. A person with a lot of influence over material and earthly matters. Behaviors that are done at a specific time. Ritual behavior or bad habits. The judgement of the damned. Your deeds create your future. Taking responsibility for your downfalls. The forgiveness of sin. Can be baptism through fire. Trials by fire. The letters F O X B K T are indicated.

The Devil (15) + The World (21)

Capricorn (Saturn + Earth) + Saturn. Saturdays during Capricorn. A lot of Saturn energy in this combination. It points to time and its effects on matter. Conquer the devil to reach completion and success. The motion of matter creates time. All colors are absorbed. Conquer selfishness and be rewarded. Every time you conquer the devil, you are rewarded. There is a time lag between good karma and bad karma. If you do something good today, you may not see the results until 10 years from now! Anything involving time. Anything infinite or eternal. The Eternal nature of the soul and the forces of evil moving throughout time. The orbit of the planets. It can be caves and dark abandoned places. Watches and watchmakers. Greed and avarice. The letters F O X C L U are indicated. These two cards are strongly linked through the planet Saturn.

The Tower (16) + The Star (17)

Mars + Aquarius (Saturn + Air) Tuesdays during Aquarius. The sudden loss of faith. Impulsive and unpredictable behavior. Angry or violent thoughts that lead to depression. Chaotic and random thoughts. Confusion. It is the electrical activity of the brain. Bad karma and the loss of hope. Giving up mentally. Aggressive thoughts. Events from the past that are still having negative results for the present. Lack of faith in the future. Competitive thoughts and a heightened state of awareness. Anger that leads to mental confusion. Batteries. Radio waves. The letters G P Y H Q Z are indicated.

The Tower (16) + The Moon (18)

Mars + Pisces (Jupiter + Water) Tuesdays during Pisces. An unexpected emotional revelation. Powerful psychic energy. Violent activity at night. Beware of deception that brings sudden loss. A fire under the light of the moon. Problems with anger. Emotional disturbances. Someone who is impulsive and changes emotions frequently. A difficult and dangerous project with very positive beneficial results. It is worth the danger! Static electricity. The electrical and magnetic effects of emotional energy. Electromagnets. An emotional climax. Dangerous, fast moving water. Self-inflicted injuries. Adrenaline. Chaos and confusion. Someone who is unsure of their emotions. The letters G P Y I R are indicated.

The Tower (16) + The Sun (19)

Mars + The Sun Two fiery, active planets. Of course Mars orbits around the Sun. The Sun gives off light and energy. The Tower is the plasma and electromagnetic solar waves that interact with the earth. Solar flares. This is heat and lightening. A daytime thunderstorm. An unplanned or unexpected pregnancy. Gold and abundance that was unpredictable. Happiness, success and abundance may be suddenly lost. It can be an unexpected disaster that destroys productivity and achievement. An accident. Competitions under the light of the sun. This combination represents activities that are spontaneous and unplanned. A positive outcome after a struggle. Solar Energy. A negative event that turns out to be a blessing. Electricity created from solar energy. The letters G P Y A J S are indicated.

The Tower (16) + Judgement (20)

Mars + Fire Nuclear war. Fire and bombs! It is the unexpected fiery attack of the enemy. It is danger. It is the punishment of hell for sinners. The destruction and fire of war. It is male aggression and violent behavior. Fighting, boxing and wrestling. Any type of martial arts. Masculine aggressive behavior. The destruction of the body so the spirit can be set free. It is rebirth after destruction. Time for physical activity and working out. There is danger of a destructive fire. Sins that have been forgiven. The fall of the angels. Cultural differences and conflicts. The letters G P Y B K T are indicated.

The Tower (16) + The World (21)

Mars | Saturn Entropy. The natural destructive power of time. The cycles of destruction that happens throughout time. It is lightening and the force of electricity. A blacksmith. Unexpected changes to fortune. An empire that has been stable for a long time will fall. Even a diamond will return to graphite over time. It is the natural chaos of matter. It is randomness. Success and rewards suddenly lost. Ruin and loss right before assured success. Bad luck and failure at the last moment. A big project that is lost. An opportunity squandered. It can point to unexpected financial gain or opportunity if well dignified. Unexpected delays. Rejection and revenge. The letters G P Y C L U are indicated.

The Star (17) + The Moon (18)

Aquarius (Saturn + Air) + Pisces (Jupiter + Water) Thursdays during Aquarius and Saturdays during Pisces are the active days. Combining thought and emotion to create something that will stand the test of time. Building a positive reputation. Becoming educated and in touch with the emotions. Having faith and contacting spiritual forces. The use of Holy Water. Baptisms. The Cusp of Aquarius and Pisces (February 21st) is indicated. Be cautious of new opportunities. Do your homework before embarking on a new adventure. Trust your instincts and be cautious. Focusing the mind to solve a complicated problem. The wave nature of time. Moments when time seems to speed up or slow down. Cyclic rhythms of the mind and thought. Patterns of thought built up over time. Habits and obsessive behaviors. A feeling of deja-vu. The letters H Q Z I R are indicated.

The Star (17) + The Sun (19)

Aquarius (Saturn + Air) + The Sun Sundays during Aquarius. It is how your knowledge becomes wisdom over time. It represents eternal truth. The evolution of the personality. Things that have been true since you were born. It is hope, healing and opportunity. These are positive thoughts and memories that you have had for a long time. It is an idea that is growing stronger over time. More and more ideas and thoughts are coming to you. Thoughts will bring opportunities. Try to take a new perspective on your life. Spend more time in contemplation and analysis of your life. Friendship. Remember, a star is really a sun that is far away. It is a change of perspective. The Sabbath. Longevity and vitality. The letters H Q Z A J S are indicated.

The Star (17) + Judgement (20)

Aquarius (Saturn + Air) + Fire Actions that are planned out well in advance. Taking action on your ideas for the future. Taking actions that prepare you for the future. Planning an event. Hopes are renewed. Opportunities are altered. Adjustments made to your future strategy. An intelligent person with good decision making skills. Someone who can adapt to changing situations quickly. It is the speed of light. It is the time lag between thought and deed. It is the time difference between actions and consequences. Motion creates time. The letters H Q Z B K T are indicated.

The Star (17) + The World (21)

Aquarius (Saturn + Air) + Saturn Saturdays during Aquarius. Time and thought. The effects of time on thought. The length of time that you can hold a thought. Thinking about something for a long time. Manifestation through concentration and faith. Manifestation based on intense focused thought. The ability to time-travel in your mind. Positive and successful opportunities. A favorable destiny is certain. A sense of good timing. Someone who is never late. Life is eternal. An intelligent and successful person with a good sense of timing. A recently plowed field. The Sabbath. Someone who is in denial. A cynic. The letters H Q Z C L U are indicated. These two cards are linked strongly through the planet Saturn.

The Moon (18) + The Sun (19)

Pisces (Jupiter + Water) + Sun. Sundays during Pisces. An eclipse. The union of the conscious and unconscious minds. Becoming conscious of your dreams. Jupiter = creation and the Sun = growth, and water is emotion. It can point to sperm and the moment of conception. Emotionally mature and balanced. Empathetic, altruistic. A psychologist may be indicated. Hypnosis and learning from dreams. Gain from a dream made conscious. Trusting your emotional instincts. An accidental success or a miracle cure for depression. Reflection and mirrors. Riches found beneath the sea. A treasure at sea that is found. A faith healer. The power of mind over matter. The letters I R A J S are indicated.

The Moon (18) + Judgement (20)

Pisces (Jupiter + Water) + Fire. Dreams and ideas that are brought back into memory. Old ideas and dreams that are brought back to life. Cycles of behavior. Constructive behaviors motivated by emotions. Protective behaviors. Being cautious. Constructive emotions and behaviors. Be cautious of major changes or upheavals. The best defense is a good offense. Someone whose destiny is in the hands of another. The creation of a spiritual body. Astral travel. The use of the imagination. Resurrection and reincarnation. The effects of moonlight on the spirit and unconscious mind. Natural moon cycles and their effects on the physical body and behavior. Light and heat that is reflected. Constructive behaviors that yield a positive emotional response. The letters I R B K T are indicated.

The Moon (18) + The World (21)

Pisces (Jupiter + Water) + Saturn Saturdays during Pisces are indicated. Manifestation using psychic energy. Images and dreams that come true. Spiritual energy that is made manifest in physical form. The completion of a task. An accomplishment that took a long time to achieve. Obstacles are overcome due to the proper emotional state of mind. The emotional investment necessary to complete a work. Beware of success. Be cautious with accomplishments. Do not let them change you too much. This combination is the gravitational force between the moon and the earth and its effects on tides and water. This combination can also point to glaciers or icicles. It is an icy formation or an ice sculpture. Poverty. Natural cycles and the seasons of the year. The letters I R C L U are indicated.

The Sun (19) + Judgement (20)

Sun + Fire. This has a similar energy as the Strength card (Leo). Growth through spiritual strength. Overcoming death, resurrection. Conquering death and disease. Successful changes. Major life changes will bring happiness. Forgiveness will bring success. Heat and danger of sunburn is indicated. Ideas from the past will bring gold and abundance. The heat of fire. Deserts and very hot places. Furnaces. Behaviors that lead to growth. Revelation through action. Learning by doing. Rebirth and a fresh start. The soul is reborn. This combination points to spiritual evolution. Generosity and redemption. The letters A J S B K T are indicated.

The Sun (19) + The World (21)

The Sun + Saturn The effect of time on energy and creation. Saturday night at midnight. Creation involves motion which creates time. The movements of the Sun are used to measure time and mark the seasons. Success is assured. Abundance, happiness and success. A positive reward. Productive success. It is growth and expansion that is recognized. It is the completion of the race in first place. The gold medal. Proper timing will bring a golden opportunity. Do not react too late or too soon or you might miss an opportunity. Vitality, time and expansion. The use of the sun or shadows to tell time. Healing that takes a long time. Riches found in the earth. A gold mine. Light and shadow. Long lasting friendships. The letters A J S C L U are indicated.

Judgement (20) + The World (21)

Fire + Saturn. It is the effects of time on behaviors. It represents habits that you have had for a long time. It is patterns of behaviors. It is how behaviors and actions affect time. Your will can be manifest, it is a matter of timing. The timing of actions is important. This combination points to evolution. Practice makes perfect. Your actions will determine how long it will take. It will not just fall into your lap, action is needed. Ideas from the past must be brought back to life by you in order to achieve your long term goals. Nobody will do it for you, so get started! Forgiveness will bring great long term rewards. It is a time of successful change. The ability to discover your relationship to the rest of the greater universe. This is the goal of life. The letters B K T C L U are indicated.

BIBLIOGRAPHY

Bills, Rex E., *The Rulership Book; A Dictionary of Astrological Correspondences*

Case, Paul Foster, *The Tarot*

Crowley, Aleister, *The Book of Thoth*

Denning, Melita and Osborne Phillips, *The Magick of the Tarot*

DeVore, Nicholas, *Encyclopedia of Astrology*

Doane, Doris Chase and King Keyes, *How to Read Tarot Cards*

Elbertin, Reinhold, *The Combination of Stellar Influences*

Garen, Nancy, *Tarot Made Easy*

Hall, Manly P., *Astrological Keywords*

Kelly, Dorothy, *Tarot Card combinations*

Regardie, Israel, *The Golden Dawn*

Rudhyar, Dane, *The Astrology of Personality*

Sadhu, Mouni, *The Tarot*

Turnbull, Coulson, *The Divine Language of Celestial Correspondences*

Waite, A. E., *Pictorial Key to the Tarot*

Wang, Robert, *The Qaballistic Tarot*

BIOGRAPHY

Kenneth has been a Tarot reader since he received his first deck of Tarot cards from his grandmother on his thirteenth birthday. His well-worn deck of Rider-Waite Tarot cards has been around the world with him and back. He has had them by his side since he received them. Kenneth uses the Tarot every day, helping real-world clients in an efficient, effective way.

Kenneth has over thirty years of experience with the Tarot cards. He has read hundreds of Tarot books over the years. He has a degree in chemistry and mathematics, and he analyzes the Tarot cards in a scientific way. He does Tarot readings by e-mail, telephone, and chat (both online and face-to-face).

This is Kenneth's first attempt at writing a book and perhaps there are more to come.

Because Kenneth was interested in Computers and Tarot, this led to the creation of his Tarot website. http://www.SunMoonTarot.com

Kenneth is available if you are interested in scheduling a Tarot reading. Contact him today!

SunMoonTarot.com